CliffsNotes™

Animal Farm

By Daniel Moran, M.A.

IN THIS BOOK

- Learn about the Life and Background of the Author
- Preview an Introduction to the Novel
- Study a graphical Character Map
- Explore themes and literary devices in the Critical Commentaries
- Examine in-depth Character Analyses
- Enhance your understanding of the work with Critical Essays
- Reinforce what you learn with CliffsNotes Review
- Find additional information to further your study in CliffsNotes Resource Center and online at www.cliffsnotes.com

WILEY

Wiley Publishing, Inc.

About the Author
   Daniel Moran is an award-winning high school
   English teacher who has also written the Cliffs-
   Notes for *The Once and Future King* and *Heart of
   Darkness*.

Publisher's Acknowledgments
Editorial
   Project Editor: Tracy Barr
   Acquisitions Editor: Greg Tubach
   Glossary Editors: The editors and staff at
   Webster's New World™ Dictionaries
   Editorial Administrator: Michelle Hacker
Composition
   Indexer: York Production Services, Inc.
   Proofreader: York Production Services, Inc.
   Wiley Indianapolis Composition Servicess

CliffsNotes™ *Animal Farm*

Published by:
Wiley Publishing, Inc.
111 River Street
Hoboken, NJ 07030
www.wiley.com

Copyright © 2001 Wiley Publishing, Inc., Hoboken, NJ
Library of Congress Control Number: 00-107702
ISBN: 978-0-7645-8669-9
Printed in the United States of America
17 16 15 14 13 12 11
1O/TQ/QZ/QW/IN
Published by Wiley Publishing, Inc., Hoboken, NJ
Published simultaneously in Canada

Table of Contents

How to Use This Book

This CliffsNotes study guide on George Orwell's *Animal Farm* supplements the original literary work, giving you background information about the author, an introduction to the work, a graphical character map, critical commentaries, expanded glossaries, and a comprehensive index, all for you to use as an educational tool that will allow you to better understand *Animal Farm*. This study guide was written with the assumption that you have read *Animal Farm*. Reading a literary work doesn't mean that you immediately grasp the major themes and devices used by the author; this study guide will help supplement your reading to be sure you get all you can from George Orwell's *Animal Farm*. CliffsNotes Review tests your comprehension of the original text and reinforces learning with questions and answers, practice projects, and more. For further information on George Orwell and *Animal Farm*, check out the CliffsNotes Resource Center.

CliffsNotes provides the following icons to highlight essential elements of particular interest:

Reveals the underlying themes in the work.

Helps you to more easily relate to or discover the depth of a character.

Uncovers elements such as setting, atmosphere, mystery, passion, violence, irony, symbolism, tragedy, foreshadowing, and satire.

Enables you to appreciate the nuances of words and phrases.

Don't Miss Our Web Site

Discover classic literature as well as modern-day treasures by visiting the Cliffs-Notes Web site at www.cliffsnotes.com. You can obtain a quick download of a CliffsNotes title, purchase a title in print form, browse our catalog, or view online samples.

LIFE AND BACKGROUND OF THE AUTHOR

The following abbreviated biography of George Orwell is provided so that you might become more familiar with his life and the historical times that possibly influenced his writing. Read this Life and Background of the Author section and recall it when reading Orwell's *Animal Farm*, thinking of any thematic relationship between Orwell's novel and his life.

Son and Student

George Orwell was born Eric Arthur Blair on June 25, 1903, in Bengal, India, where his father, Richard Walmesley Blair, was an official in the Opium Department. Like many middle-to-upper-class men of his time, Richard Blair served the British Empire in its most prized and lucrative colony. In 1896, he met Ida Amble Limouzin, a British governess 20 years his junior, also living in India. After their marriage, the couple lived in Bengal for eight years, where they had two children: Marjorie (born 1898) and Eric. One year after Eric's birth, Ida moved back to England. For the next eight years, Eric would see his father for only three months in 1907, during one of his leaves. A third child, Avril, was born in 1908. Richard did not see his youngest child until his return to England when he retired from the Opium Department in 1912.

Eric spent his early boyhood in Henley, Oxfordshire, where he was an admittedly "chubby boy" who enjoyed walks in the Oxfordshire countryside. During this time, he began to vaguely understand his family's need to spend money to "keep up appearances" and the differences between members of different social classes: A friendship with a plumber's daughter was broken by his mother because she found the girl "too common." Not surprisingly, Eric was enthralled with books, notably Jonathan Swift's *Gulliver's Travels*—a novel whose political satire would find its way into the books of George Orwell.

In the summer of 1911, Eric entered into the defining phase of his childhood when he was admitted to St. Cyprian's, a preparatory school in Eastbourne with a reputation for readying boys for notable "public" (that is, private) schools. He began his first term there in 1912 and, until he left it five years later, almost wholly dreaded and hated the experience. He was humiliated as a bed wetter, forced to memorize streams of dates and names, mocked by the wealthier boys, and led to believe that (in his own words), "[l]ife was more terrible, and I was more wicked, than I had imagined." The headmaster and his wife routinely reminded Eric that he was attending their school on a partial scholarship in order to shame him into behaving as they wished—this was another lesson to young Eric about the importance of social class and money. His years at St. Cyprian's are described at length in his essay, "Such, Such, Were the Joys . . . " (1952), and a reader of the essay can see that it was at St. Cyprian's that Orwell began to truly recognize the ways in which the strong belittle, control, and terrorize the weak—an idea that would later inform his political views and two most renowned novels, *Animal Farm* and *Nineteen Eighty-Four*. Although Orwell did enjoy some of his time at St. Cyprians (collecting butterflies, for example), he yearned for the escape he finally achieved when his impressive grades earned him a scholarship at Wellington College, where he went in 1916.

After spending only nine weeks at Wellington, however, Eric learned that he had been accepted to Eton—one of the nation's most prestigious schools—as a King's Scholar, whose education was almost entirely paid for by a scholarship. Eric's grades at Eton were unimpressive, although he did read a great deal, especially modern writers like Jack London, H. G. Wells, and George Bernard Shaw, who undoubtedly helped Eric shape his growing social consciousness. Eton was also the place where Eric began to write seriously, although what remains from this period is largely juvenilia. In December of 1921, Eric graduated from Eton, and although many Eton boys continued their studies at Oxford or Cambridge, Eric's marks were too low for him to receive a scholarship. His father (understandably) refused to pay for more schooling if Eric was not prepared to perform. Facing an undecided future, the 18-year-old Eric Blair made a decision that would heighten his awareness of politics and the abuses of power done in the name of goodness and moral virtue.

Officer and Tramp

If Eric could not become a scholar, he knew that he had a good chance at becoming a servant of the Empire which had employed his father for 30 years. He announced to his parents that he wanted to become a police officer in India, and they approved. Inspired by the status of the position, the good wages he would earn, and perhaps by a desire to see remote parts of the world, Orwell took and passed the admission test for the Imperial Police. When asked to name the Indian province to which he would most like to be assigned, Eric requested Burma—a shocking answer for a man his age, since Burma was an often lawless place, high on crime but low on comforts. He had little experience as a soldier (save for the Officer Training Corps at Eton) and none in a police force. There was also a great amount of tension in Burma between the British and Indian populations. Despite these apparent deterrents, in November, 1922, Eric arrived in Mandalay, Burma, to begin his new career as an Assistant Superintendent of Police in the Indian Imperial Police Force.

While in Burma, Eric developed a great distaste for the British rule of India and for imperialism altogether. As a police officer, he was expected to maintain order in a population that detested him. In turn, he also sometimes hated those he was being paid to protect. As he describes in "Shooting an Elephant" (1936), imperialism destroys both the rulers and the ruled: "I was stuck between my hatred of the empire I served and the evil-spirited little beasts who tried to make my job impossible." His experiences in Burma would find their way into his essay "A Hanging" (1931) and his first novel, *Burmese Days* (1934). He resigned from the Indian Imperial Police Force in 1928 and returned to England, a 25-five year-old determined to become a writer able to comment on his ever-growing political consciousness.

To find material for his writing and learn about the lives of the lower classes, Eric began "tramping" through London and Paris. Fascinated by the lives of the poor and by the fact that a nation as powerful as England could fail to address such shocking poverty, Eric lived among the lower classes, although he could have stayed in his parents' comfortable home. Dressed in shoddy clothes, Eric would sit on street corners, converse with tramps, and spend time in the various "spikes" (men's shelters provided by factories) around London. In Paris, he took a job as a *plongeur* (a dishwasher) and learned more about the suffering of the poor in another European capital. While in Paris, he contracted pneumonia and spent three weeks in the public ward of the Hopital Cochin—a depressing but enlightening experience that he later recorded in the essay, "How the Poor Die." (Problems with his lungs plagued him his entire life.)

His experiences were shaped into his first book, *Down and Out in Paris and London*, a work of non-fiction that Orwell asked a friend to destroy (convinced that it had no merit) but which the same friend took to an agent, who in turn took it to a publisher. *Down and Out* was published in 1933 to good reviews—reviews that spoke of the author not as "Eric Blair," but as "George Orwell," a pseudonym Eric chose in case the book was a total failure. For the remainder of his career, he remained Orwell to his readers but Eric to his family and friends.

Novelist and Soldier

During the early and mid-1930s, Orwell dabbled in teaching while trying to sustain himself as a writer. His novels *Burmese Days* (1934), *A Clergyman's Daughter* (1935), and *Keep the Aspidistra Flying* (1936) all met with decent reviews but modest sales. In 1936, Orwell employed the same method he had used to write *Down and Out* and visited Wigan, a mining town in Northern England, to see how the miners and their families lived. The result was *The Road to Wigan Pier* (1937), a non-fictional account of the miners' struggles that was chosen by the Left Book Club and sold over 44,000 copies. Orwell was now regarded as an important political writer, much more so than as a novelist. This same year also saw Orwell become a husband: On June 9, 1936, he married Eileen O'Shaughnessy.

Orwell and his new wife did not begin a peaceful married life; rather, they both traveled to Spain to serve in the fight against fascism which would become the Spanish Civil War. Orwell left England in December of 1936 and served in the P. O. U. M. (The Worker's Party of Marxist Unification)—a socialist party allied with England's Independent Labour Party (I. L. P.). Orwell was responsible for training a band of Catalonian soldiers fighting General Franco on the Aragon front. Eileen arrived in Barcelona in February of 1937 to serve as a typist for the I. L. P.'s Spanish offices. That May, Orwell was hit by a sniper in the throat but miraculously lived and only lost the use of his voice for a few weeks. Eventually, the P. O. U. M. was outlawed by the more powerful communist forces that arose as a result of the conflict, and Orwell escaped (with Eileen) to France after serving more than three months in combat. *Homage to Catalonia* (1938), another non-fiction work, describes Orwell's time on the front and his disillusionment with the very revolution he thought would win freedom for Spain. This idea of a revolution betraying its supposed aims is a chief issue of *Animal Farm*.

Napoleon and Big Brother

After returning from France, Orwell's lungs began troubling him again; he was showing signs of tuberculosis and was admitted to a sanatorium in Kent, where he convalesced for four months before leaving for Marrakech, Morocco—a spot chosen because of the supposed recuperative effects of its climate. In Marrakech, he wrote another novel, *Coming Up for Air* (1939) and then returned, in 1939, to London. World War II erupted and Orwell continued writing reviews, essays, and broadcasts to India from the BBC. Non-fiction works from this period include *Inside the Whale* (1940) and *The Lion and the Unicorn* (1941).

In 1943, Orwell finished writing the book that would seal his reputation as an insightful and cautious political thinker: *Animal Farm*. Dubbed "A Fairy Story," Orwell's short but powerful novel examines the ways in which a farm of oppressed and exploited animals rebel against their human master, only to eventually replace the system they initially wanted to supplant. The book is also a thinly disguised retelling of the 1917 Russian Revolution from Orwell's point-of-view. Because of this, the book was rejected by several publishers on the grounds that it was too controversial to publish at a time when the Soviets were at war with Germany—the wartime enemy of England. While negotiations on *Animal Farm* were still pending, Orwell and Eileen adopted a son, Richard Horatio, in 1944. *Animal Farm* was finally published on August 17, 1945, sold more than 250,000 copies, and received tremendously flattering reviews. However, with this great success came sorrow, when Eileen died during a hysterectomy this same year.

In 1947, Orwell moved to Jura, an island off the coast of Scotland. Here he composed the novel which proved to be his most enduring work: *Nineteen Eighty-Four*. Published in 1949, the novel evokes a nightmarish future where the citizens of "Oceania" are totally controlled by the Party, a political machine symbolized by the mythical figure Big Brother. Orwell's lungs, however, were getting worse. Just before his death, he married the young editorial assistant Sonia Brownwell in a University Hospital bedside ceremony on October 13, 1949. Orwell died of tuberculosis on January 21, 1950, but his contributions to political literature—best seen in the fact that the adjective "Orwellian" has come into the language—remain.

INTRODUCTION TO THE NOVEL

   The following Introduction section is provided solely as an educational tool and is not meant to replace the experience of your reading the novel. Read the Introduction and A Brief Synopsis to enhance your understanding of the novel and to prepare yourself for the critical thinking that should take place whenever you read any work of fiction or non-fiction. Keep the List of Characters and Character Map at hand so that as you read the original literary work, if you encounter a character about whom you're uncertain, you can refer to the List of Characters and Character Map to refresh your memory.

Introduction

As Orwell spent more and more time with the down-and-outs of England, he became convinced that the only remedy for the invidious problem of poverty lay in socialism, a political and economic philosophy arguing that only when the state controls the means of production and distribution will all members of a nation share its profits and rewards. Unlike capitalism, the philosophy holding that a nation's means of production and distribution should be privately owned and controlled, socialism argues that only government regulation of a nation's economy can close the gap between the rich and the poor. Although he was not a virulent anti-capitalist, Orwell did think that only with the gradual introduction of socialist ideas and practices into British life would the poor eventually come to share in the fruits of their nation's prosperity.

As he explained in his Preface to the Ukrainian edition of *Animal Farm*, "I became pro-Socialist more out of disgust with the way the poorer section of the industrial workers were oppressed and neglected than out of any theoretical admiration for a planned society." After fighting against fascism (an oppressive system of government in which the ruling party has complete economic control) in the Spanish Civil War, Orwell dedicated himself to exploring political questions in his writing. As he explains in the essay "Why I Write," "Every line of serious work I have written since 1936 has been written, directly or indirectly, *against* totalitarianism and *for* democratic socialism." His detestation and fear of totalitarianism—an even more extreme form of fascism in which the ruling party has complete control over all aspects of a people's lives—thus informed much of his literary output.

Orwell examined socialism in a number of his nonfiction works but was prompted to write *Animal Farm* by what he saw as a prevalent—and false—belief that the Russian Revolution of 1917 was a step toward socialism for millions of poor and oppressed Russians. Orwell felt that Stalin's brutal rise to power was not only barbaric, but a betrayal of the socialist principles for which Lenin, Trotsky, and he had presumably revolted. In hindsight, this seems obvious, but in the world of World War II Europe, such an attack on Russia was willingly stifled by many British leftists who wanted to believe that Russia was indeed moving toward a true union of socialist republics. The fact that Russia was—like England—fighting Hitler also made Orwell's position more unpalatable to leftist thinkers. Still, he felt that the U.S.S.R. was not progressing toward socialism but totalitarianism: "I was struck by clear signs of its transformation into a hierarchical society, in which the rulers have no more reason to give up their power than any ruling class." Convinced that "a destruction of the Soviet myth was essential if we wanted a revival of the Socialist movement," Orwell began thinking about how he could best communicate his opinions on socialism and Stalin.

His thoughts were ignited when he happened to see a village boy whipping a cart-horse. At that moment, Orwell received the inspiration he needed to formulate his ideas into *Animal Farm*: "It struck me that if only such animals became aware of their strength we would have no power over them, and that men exploit animals" as the government in a totalitarian state exploits the common people. Now Orwell had a plan for his novel which would both argue the need for a true socialist government and warn the world of the ways in which socialist ideas threatened the will of these in power who wish to control other people. His book would demonstrate the ways in which—despite all of their socialist propaganda—the leaders of the Russian Revolution (especially Stalin) had created in a system even worse than its previous one and sound an alarm to all English readers about the dangers of believing in the Soviet myth. (For a more detailed examination of how the events of the novel parallel those of the Russian Revolution, see the Critical Essays.) After a number of rejections from publishers, the novel was finally accepted by the small publishing firm of Secker and Warburg and proved to be a tremendous success, both in England and the United States. After *Nineteen Eighty-Four*, another novel that portrays life under an oppressive government, *Animal Farm* is Orwell's most renowned work.

Of course, the novel's meaning is not rooted solely in its portrayal of the Russian Revolution. The novel asks its readers to examine the ways in which political leaders with seemingly noble and altruistic motives can betray the very ideals in which they ostensibly believe, as well as the ways in which certain members of a nation can elect themselves to positions of great power and abuse their fellow citizens, all under the guise of assisting them. The novel also presents the subtle ways in which a group of citizens—of a farm or a nation—can be eventually led by the nose into a terrible life ruled by a totalitarian regime. In "Why I Write," Orwell describes *Animal Farm* as "the first book in which I tried, with full consciousness of what I was doing, to fuse political purpose and artistic purpose into one whole." His political purpose—presenting a model of socialism gone wrong—is found in the way that the novel's animals reflect different kinds of humans and their struggles for freedom and power. Orwell felt that a farm where "All Animals Are Equal" would solve many social and economic problems—but he also knew that such a system would be difficult to maintain, since some animals would act on the principle that "Some Are More Equal Than Others."

A Brief Synopsis

One night, all the animals at Mr. Jones' Manor Farm assemble in a barn to hear old Major, a pig, describe a dream he had about a world where all animals live free from the tyranny of their human masters. Old Major dies soon after the meeting, but the animals—inspired by his philosophy of Animalism—plot a rebellion against Jones. Two pigs, Snowball and Napoleon, prove themselves important figures and planners of this dangerous enterprise. When Jones forgets to feed the animals, the revolution occurs, and Jones and his men are chased off the farm. Manor Farm is renamed Animal Farm, and the Seven Commandments of Animalism are painted on the barn wall.

Initially, the rebellion is a success: The animals complete the harvest and meet every Sunday to debate farm policy. The pigs, because of their intelligence, become the supervisors of the farm. Napoleon, however, proves to be a power-hungry leader who steals the cows' milk and a number of apples to feed himself and the other pigs. He also enlists the services of Squealer, a pig with the ability to persuade the other animals that the pigs are always moral and correct in their decisions.

Later that fall, Jones and his men return to Animal Farm and attempt to retake it. Thanks to the tactics of Snowball, the animals defeat Jones in what thereafter becomes known as The Battle of the Cowshed. Winter arrives, and Mollie, a vain horse concerned only with ribbons and sugar, is lured off the farm by another human. Snowball begins drawing plans for a windmill, which will provide electricity and thereby give the animals more leisure time, but Napoleon vehemently opposes such a plan on the grounds that building the windmill will allow them less time for producing food. On the Sunday that the pigs offer the windmill to the animals for a vote, Napoleon summons a pack of ferocious dogs, who chase Snowball off the farm forever. Napoleon announces that there will be no further debates; he also tells them that the windmill will be built after all and lies that it was his own idea, stolen by Snowball. For the rest of the novel, Napoleon uses Snowball as a scapegoat on whom he blames all of the animals' hardships.

Much of the next year is spent building the windmill. Boxer, an incredibly strong horse, proves himself to be the most valuable animal in this endeavor. Jones, meanwhile, forsakes the farm and moves to another part of the county. Contrary to the principles of Animalism, Napoleon hires a solicitor and begins trading with neighboring farms. When a storm topples the half-finished windmill, Napoleon predictably blames Snowball and orders the animals to begin rebuilding it.

Napoleon's lust for power increases to the point where he becomes a totalitarian dictator, forcing "confessions" from innocent animals and having the dogs kill them in front of the entire farm. He and the pigs move into Jones' house and begin sleeping in beds (which Squealer excuses with his brand of twisted logic). The animals receive less and less food, while the pigs grow fatter. After the windmill is completed in August, Napoleon sells a pile of timber to Frederick, a neighboring farmer who pays for it with forged banknotes. Frederick and his men attack the farm and explode the windmill but are eventually defeated. As more of the Seven Commandments of Animalism are broken by the pigs, the language of the Commandments is revised: For example, after the pigs become drunk one night, the Commandment, "No animals shall drink alcohol" is changed to, "No animal shall drink alcohol to excess."

Boxer again offers his strength to help build a new windmill, but when he collapses, exhausted, Napoleon sells the devoted horse to a knacker (a glue-boiler). Squealer tells the indignant animals that Boxer was actually taken to a veterinarian and died a peaceful death in a hospital—a tale the animals believe.

Years pass and Animal Farm expands its boundaries after Napoleon purchases two fields from another neighboring farmer, Pilkington. Life for all the animals (except the pigs) is harsh. Eventually, the pigs begin walking on their hind legs and take on many other qualities of their former human oppressors. The Seven Commandments are reduced to a single law: "All Animals Are Equal / But Some Are More Equal Than Others." The novel ends with Pilkington sharing drinks with the pigs in Jones' house. Napoleon changes the name of the farm back to Manor Farm and quarrels with Pilkington during a card game in which both of them try to play the ace of spades. As other animals watch the scene from outside the window, they cannot tell the pigs from the humans.

List of Characters

The Animals

Major An old boar whose speech about the evils perpetrated by humans rouses the animals into rebelling. His philosophy concerning the tyranny of Man is named Animalism by his followers. He also teaches the song "Beasts of England" to the animals.

Snowball A boar who becomes one of the rebellion's most valuable leaders. After drawing complicated plans for the construction of a windmill, he is chased off of the farm forever by Napoleon's dogs and thereafter used as a scapegoat for the animals' troubles.

Napoleon A boar who, with Snowball, leads the rebellion against Jones. After the rebellion's success, he systematically begins to control all aspects of the farm until he is an undisputed tyrant.

Squealer A porker pig who becomes Napoleon's mouthpiece. Throughout the novel, he displays his ability to manipulate the animals' thoughts through the use of hollow yet convincing rhetoric.

Boxer A dedicated but dimwitted horse who aids in the building of the windmill but is sold to a glue-boiler after collapsing from exhaustion.

Mollie A vain horse who prefers ribbons and sugar over ideas and rebellion. She is eventually lured off the farm with promises of a comfortable life.

Clover A motherly horse who silently questions some of Napoleon's decisions and tries to help Boxer after his collapse.

Benjamin A cynical, pessimistic donkey who continually undercuts the animals' enthusiasm with his cryptic remark, "Donkeys live a long time."

Moses   A tame raven and sometimes-pet of Jones who tells the animals stories about a paradise called Sugarcandy Mountain.

Bluebell, Jessie, and Pincher   Three dogs. The nine puppies born between Jessie and Bluebell are taken by Napoleon and raised to be his guard dogs.

The Humans

Mr. Jones   The often-drunk owner of Manor Farm, later expelled from his land by his own animals. He dies in an inebriates' home after abandoning his hopes to reclaim his farm.

Mrs. Jones   Jones' wife, who flees from the farm when the animals rebel.

Mr. Whymper   A solicitor hired by Napoleon to act as an intermediary in Animal Farm's trading with neighboring farms.

Mr. Pilkington   The owner of Foxwood, a neighboring and neglected farm. He eventually sells some of his land to Napoleon and, in the novel's final scene, toasts to Napoleon's success.

Mr. Frederick   An enemy of Pilkington and owner of Pinchfield, another neighboring farm. Known for "driving hard bargains," Frederick swindles Napoleon by buying timber from him with counterfeit money. He later tries to attack and seize Animal Farm but is defeated.

Character Map

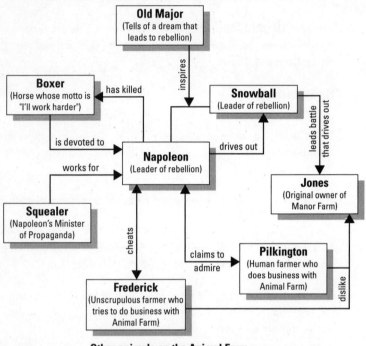

Old Major
(Tells of a dream that leads to rebellion)

inspires

Boxer
(Horse whose motto is "I'll work harder")

has killed

Snowball
(Leader of rebellion)

leads battle that drives out

is devoted to

Napoleon
(Leader of rebellion)

drives out

works for

Jones
(Original owner of Manor Farm)

Squealer
(Napoleon's Minister of Propaganda)

cheats

Pilkington
(Human farmer who does business with Animal Farm)

claims to admire

dislike

Frederick
(Unscrupulous farmer who tries to do business with Animal Farm)

Other animals on the Animal Farm

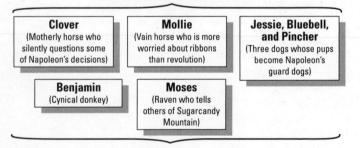

Clover
(Motherly horse who silently questions some of Napoleon's decisions)

Mollie
(Vain horse who is more worried about ribbons than revolution)

Jessie, Bluebell, and Pincher
(Three dogs whose pups become Napoleon's guard dogs)

Benjamin
(Cynical donkey)

Moses
(Raven who tells others of Sugarcandy Mountain)

CRITICAL COMMENTARIES

The sections that follow provide great tools for supplementing your reading of *Animal Farm*. First, in order to enhance your understanding of and enjoyment from reading, we provide quick summaries in case you have difficulty when you read the original literary work. Each summary is followed by commentary: literary devices, character analyses, themes, and so on. Keep in mind that the interpretations here are solely those of the author of this study guide and are used to jumpstart your thinking about the work. No single interpretation of a complex work like *Animal Farm* is infallible or exhaustive, and you'll likely find that you interpret portions of the work differently from the author of this study guide. Read the original work and determine your own interpretations, referring to these Notes for supplemental meanings only.

Chapter 1

Summary

After Mr. Jones, the owner of Manor Farm, falls asleep in a drunken stupor, all of his animals meet in the big barn at the request of old Major, a 12-year-old pig. Major delivers a rousing political speech about the evils inflicted upon them by their human keepers and their need to rebel against the tyranny of Man. After elaborating on the various ways that Man has exploited and harmed the animals, Major mentions a strange dream of his in which he saw a vision of the earth without humans. He then teaches the animals a song—"Beasts of England"—which they sing repeatedly until they awaken Jones, who fires his gun from his bedroom window, thinking there is a fox in the yard. Frightened by the shot, the animals disperse and go to sleep.

Commentary

Character Insight

Several of the novel's main characters are introduced in this chapter; Orwell paints their dominant characteristics with broad strokes. Jones, for example, is presented as a drunken, careless ruler, whose drinking belies the upscale impression he hopes to create with the name of his farm. In addition, Jones' very name (a common one) suggests he is like many other humans, and the tyranny of all mankind is an important theme of Major's speech. His unsteady gait (suggested by the "dancing lantern" he carries) and snoring wife mark him immediately as the epitome of all that Major says about mankind's self-absorption and gluttony. Indeed, the first chapter presents Jones as more of an "animal" than the animals themselves, who reacts to any disruption of his comfort with the threat of violence, as indicated by his gunfire when he is awakened from his drunken dreams.

The animals assembling in the barn are likewise characterized by Orwell in quick fashion: Major is old and wise, Clover is motherly and sympathetic, Boxer is strong yet dimwitted, Benjamin is pessimistic and cynical, and Mollie is vain and childish. All of these characteristics become more pronounced as the novel proceeds.

However, Major's speech is the most important part of the chapter, and through it Orwell displays his great understanding of political rhetoric and how it can be used to move crowds in whichever direction the speaker wishes. By addressing his audience as "comrades" and prefacing his remarks with the statement that he will not be with the others "many months longer," Major ingratiates himself to his listeners as one who has reached a degree of wisdom in his long life of twelve years and who views the other animals as equals—not a misguided rabble that needs advice and correction from a superior intellect. This notion that "All Animals Are Equal" becomes one of the tenets of Animalism, the philosophy upon which the rebellion will supposedly be based.

Major's speech seems to initially echo the thoughts of Thomas Hobbes, the seventeenth-century English philosopher who wrote (in his work *Leviathan*) that men in an unchecked state of nature will live lives that are "poor, nasty, brutish, and short." Unlike Hobbes, however, who felt that a strong, authoritative government was required to keep everyone's innate self-interest from destroying society, Major argues that the earth could be a paradise if the tyranny of Man was overthrown; he presents his fellow animals as victims of oppression and incapable of any wrongdoing. The flaw in Major's thinking, therefore, is the assumption that only humans are capable of evil—an assumption that will be overturned as the novel progresses. Although he tells his listeners, "Remove Man from the scene, and the root cause of hunger and overwork is abolished for ever," this will not prove to be the case.

As previously mentioned, Major possesses great rhetorical skill. His barrage of rhetorical questions makes his argument more forceful, as does his imagery of the "cruel knife" and the animals screaming their "lives out at the block within a year." Major also specifically addresses Man's tyranny in terms of how he destroys families, consumes without producing, withholds food, kills the weak, and prevents them from owning even their own bodies. Major uses slogans as well ("All men are enemies. All animals are comrades.") because he knows that they are easily grasped by listeners as simpleminded as Boxer. The speech is a masterful example of persuasion, and his argument that a rebellion must take place is reminiscent of the one made by Patrick Henry to the House of Burgesses in Virginia, where he argued that a potential war with England was both inevitable and desirable.

Of course, the irony of the entire episode in the barn is that the animals will eventually betray the ideals set forth by Major. He warns, for example, that the animals must never come to resemble their human oppressors—but by the end of the novel, the tyrannical pigs are indistinguishable from their human companions. Old Major's dream of an animal utopia will quickly become a totalitarian nightmare.

The song "Beasts of England" is another way in which Major rouses his audience. Although the narrator jokes that the tune is "something between *Clementine* and *La Cucaracha*," the animals find it rousing and moving. The use of a song to stir the citizenry is an old political maneuver, and the lyrics of "Beasts of England" summarize Major's feelings about Man: The song describes a day when all animals (even Irish ones—a detail Orwell knew would resonate with a British readership) will overcome their tormentors. Symbols such as rings in their noses, harnesses, bits, spurs, and whips are used to convey the liberty that Major hopes will one day be won. Images of food and plenty also contribute to the song's appeal. The singing of this powerful piece of propaganda reflects one of the novel's chief themes: Language can be used as a weapon and means of manipulation. As the animals will later learn, characters like Napoleon and Squealer will prove even more skilled at using words to get others to do their bidding.

Glossary

(Here and in the following glossary sections, difficult words and phrases, as well as historical references and allusions, will be explained.)

tushes   tusks.

eighteen hands high   a "hand" is a four-inch unit of measurement used to describe the height of horses; eighteen hands therefore equals 72 inches.

paddock   a small field or enclosure near a stable, in which horses are exercised.

knacker   a person who buys and slaughters worn-out horses and sells their flesh as dog's meat.

Clementine and La Cucaracha   two popular folk songs.

mangel-wurzels   a variety of large beet, used as food for cattle.

Chapter 2

Summary

After the death of old Major, the animals spend their days secretly planning the rebellion, although they are unsure when it will occur. Because of their intelligence, the pigs are placed in charge of educating the animals about Animalism, the name they give to the philosophy expounded by Major in Chapter 1. Among the pigs, Snowball and Napoleon are the most important to the revolution. Despite Mollie's concern with ribbons and Moses' tales of a place called Sugarcandy Mountain, the pigs are successful in conveying the principles of Animalism to the others.

The rebellion occurs when Jones again falls into a drunken sleep and neglects to feed the animals, who break into the store-shed in search of a meal. When Jones and his men arrive, they begin whipping the animals but soon find themselves being attacked and chased off the farm. The triumphant animals then destroy all traces of Jones, eat heartily, and revel in their newfound freedom. After a tour of Jones' house, they decide to leave it untouched as a museum. Snowball changes the sign reading "Manor Farm" to "Animal Farm" and paints the Seven Commandments of Animalism on the wall of the barn. The cows then give five buckets of milk, which Napoleon steals.

Commentary

The death of old Major marks the moment when the animals must begin to put his theory into practice. For the remainder of the novel, Orwell depicts the ever-widening gulf between the vision expounded by old Major and the animals' attempt to realize it.

Character Insight

The names of the pigs chosen to lead the revolution reveal their personalities. Snowball's name suits the revolution in general, which "snowballs" and grows until, at the novel's end, the animal rulers completely resemble their previous masters. Napoleon's name suggests his stern leadership style (he has "a reputation for getting his own way") and, of course, his incredible lust for power, which becomes more pronounced with each chapter. Squealer, as his name suggests, becomes the mouthpiece of the pigs. His habit of "skipping from side to side" while arguing "some difficult point" dramatizes, in a physical way, what the smooth-talking pig will later do in a rhetorical sense: Every time he is faced with a question or objection, he will "skip" around the topic, using convoluted logic to prove his point. In short, he eventually serves as Napoleon's Minister of Propaganda.

Like all patriots and revolutionaries, Snowball is earnest and determined to win as many converts to his cause as he can. Two animals, however, momentarily fluster him. Mollie's concern over sugar and ribbons is offensive to Snowball because he (as a proponent of Animalism) urges his fellow beasts to sacrifice their luxuries. To him, Mollie is a shallow materialist, concerned only with her own image and comforts. Like Mollie, Moses proves irksome to Snowball because Moses fills the heads of the animals with tales of Sugarcandy Mountain.

What Snowball (and the rest of the animals) fail to realize is that Sugarcandy Mountain—a paradise—is as unattainable a place as a farm wholly devoted to the principles of Animalism. As the biblical Moses led his people out of bondage and into the Promised Land, Moses the raven only offers a *story* about an obviously fictitious place. The fact that the animals are so willing to believe him reveals their wish for a utopia that (in the sky or on the farm) will never be found. Thus, Moses is the novel's "religious figure," but in a strictly ironic sense, since Orwell never implies that Moses' stories better the animals' condition. As Karl Marx famously said, "Religion . . . is the opium of the people"—an idea shown in the animals' acceptance of Moses' tales.

Once the animals rebel and drive Jones from the farm, they behave as a conquering army retaking its own land and freeing it from the yoke of oppression. All the symbols of Jones' reign—nose-rings, dog-chains, knives—are tossed into a celebratory bonfire. More important is that the animals attempt to create their own sense of history and tradition by preserving Jones' house as a museum. Presumably, future animals will visit the house to learn of the terrible luxury in which humans once lived, but, like Sugarcandy Mountain, this world where all animals study their oppressors instead of *becoming* them is a fantasy. Similarly, the renaming of Manor Farm to Animal Farm suggests the animals' triumph over their enemy. By renaming the farm, they assume that they will change the kind of place it has become—another example of their optimism and innocence.

The Seven Commandments of Animalism, like the biblical Ten Commandments, are an attempt to completely codify the animals' behavior to comply with a system of morality. Like the Ten

Commandments, the Seven Commandments are direct and straight-forward, leaving no room for interpretation or qualification. The fact that they are painted in "great white letters" on the side of the barn suggests the animals' desire to make these laws permanent—as the permanence of the Ten Commandments is suggested by their being engraved on stone tablets. Of course, like the Ten Commandments, the Seven Commandments are bound to be broken and bound to be toyed with by those looking for a loophole to excuse their wrongdoing.

The chapter's final episode involving the buckets of milk hints at the ruthlessness Napoleon will display as the novel progresses. One of the hens suggests that the milk be put into the animals' mash so that all can enjoy it—an Animalistic thought, to be sure, since the Seventh Commandment of Animalism states that "All animals are equal." Note that Napoleon, however, places himself in front of the buckets and sends Snowball to lead the animals to the harvest. Already the reader can sense the boar's greed and betrayal of the most basic law of Animalism. Napoleon is using the patriotism and drive of the other animals for his own purposes, which initially involve gaining as much control over the farm's food as he can.

Glossary

porkers   hogs, especially young ones, fattened for use as food.

Windsor chair   a style of wooden chair, esp. popular in eighteenth-century England and America, with spreading legs, a back of spindles, and usually a saddle seat.

Midsummer's Eve   the night before the summer solstice, about June 21.

News of the World   a popular periodical.

carpet bag   an old-fashioned type of traveling bag, made of carpeting.

spinney   a small wood; copse.

Brussels carpet   a patterned carpeting made of small loops of colored woolen yarn in a linen warp.

Queen Victoria   1819–1901; queen of Great Britain & Ireland (1837–1901): empress of India (1876–1901): granddaughter of George III.

Chapter 3

Summary

Despite the initial difficulties inherent in using farming tools designed for humans, the animals cooperate to finish the harvest—and do so in less time than it had taken Jones and his men to do the same. Boxer distinguishes himself as a strong, tireless worker, admired by all the animals. The pigs become the supervisors and directors of the animal workers. On Sundays, the animals meet in the big barn to listen to Snowball and Napoleon debate a number of topics on which they seem never to agree. Snowball forms a number of Animal Committees, all of which fail. However, he does prove successful at bringing a degree of literacy to the animals, who learn to read according to their varied intelligences. To help the animals understand the general precepts of Animalism, Snowball reduces the Seven Commandments to a single slogan: "Four legs good, two legs bad." Napoleon, meanwhile, focuses his energy on educating the youth and takes the infant pups of Jessie and Bluebell away from their mothers, presumably for educational purposes.

The animals learn that the cows' milk and windfallen apples are mixed every day into the pigs' mash. When the animals object, Squealer explains that the pigs need the milk and apples to sustain themselves as they work for the benefit of all the other animals.

Commentary

While the successful harvest seems to signal the overall triumph of the rebellion, Orwell hints in numerous ways that the very ideals that the rebels used as their rallying cry are being betrayed by the pigs. The fact that they do not do any physical work but instead stand behind the horses shouting commands suggests their new positions as masters—and as creatures very much like the humans they presumably wanted to overthrow.

When Squealer explains to the animals why the pigs have been getting all the milk and apples, he reveals his rhetorical skill and ability to "skip from side to side" to convince the animals that the pigs' greed is actually a great sacrifice: Appealing to science (which presumably has proven that apples and milk are "absolutely necessary to the well-being of a pig") and lying about pigs disliking the very food they are hoarding, Squealer manages a great public-relations stunt by portraying the pigs as near-martyrs who only think of others and never themselves. "It is for your sake that we drink that milk and eat those apples," Squealer explains, and his dazzling pseudo-logic persuades the murmuring animals that the pigs are, in fact, selfless.

Squealer's rhetorical question, "Surely there is no one among you who wants to see Jones back?" is the first of many times when Squealer will invoke the name of Jones to convince the animals that—despite any discontentment they may feel—their present lives are greatly preferable to the ones they led under their old master. Orwell's tone when describing the animals' reaction to Squealer ("The importance of keeping the pigs in good health was all too obvious") is markedly ironic and again signals to the reader that the pigs are slowly changing into a new form of their old oppressors.

The flag created by Snowball is, like the Seven Commandments and the preserving of Jones' house as a museum, an attempt by the animals to create a greater sense of solidarity and emphasize their victory. Snowball's Animal Committees fail, however, because in them he attempts to radically transform the animals' very natures. Trying to create a "Clean Tails League" for the cows is as doomed to fail as trying to tame the wild animals in a "Wild Comrade's Re-education Committee." Snowball's aims may be noble and high-minded, but he is naive in thinking that he can alter the very nature of the animals' personalities. Thus, Snowball is marked as the intellectual theoretician of the rebellion—a characteristic that will be heightened later when he begins planning the construction of the windmill. Like old Major, Snowball has noble yet naive assumptions about the purity of animals' natures.

Unlike Snowball, Napoleon is a pig of action who cares little for committees. His assumption that the education of the young is the most important duty of the animal leaders may sound like one of Snowball's altruistic ideas—but he only says this to excuse his seizure of the new pups that he will raise to be the vicious guard dogs he uses to terrorize the farm in later chapters.

Note that the characters of other animals are further developed in this chapter. Boxer, for example, is portrayed as a simple-minded but dedicated worker: He cannot learn any more than four letters of the alphabet, but what he lacks in intelligence he more than makes up for in devotion to the farm. His new motto—"I will work harder"—and request to be called to the field half an hour before anyone else marks him as exactly the kind of animal that the pigs feel confident in controlling. When there is no thought, there can only be blind acceptance. (Like Boxer, the sheep are content with repeating a motto instead of engaging in any real thought. Their repetition of "Four legs good, two legs bad" will continue throughout the novel, usually when Napoleon needs them to quiet any dissention.)

Mollie's vanity is stressed in her reluctance to work during the harvest—she cannot devote herself to any cause other than her own ego. Thus, when she is taught to read, she refuses to learn any letters except the ones that spell her name. Unlike Snowball (and his intellectual fancies) or Napoleon (and his ruthlessness), Mollie willingly abstains from any part in the political process.

Old Benjamin's character is likewise developed in this chapter. Orwell points out that Benjamin "never changed" and that, when asked about the rebellion, only remarks, "Donkeys live a long time. None of you has ever seen a dead donkey." The other animals find this reply a "cryptic" one, but the reader understands Benjamin's point: He is wary of becoming too enthusiastic about the rebellion, since he knows that any new government can succumb to the temptation to abuse its power. Later, when the animals learn to read, Benjamin never does, since he finds "nothing worth reading." His cynicism is out-of-place with the patriotism felt by the other animals, but he cannot be convinced that the rebellion is a wholly noble cause—and, after witnessing the actions of the pigs, neither can the reader.

Glossary

cutter a small, light sleigh, usually drawn by one horse.

whelped gave birth to: said of some animals; here, meaning a litter of puppies was born.

windfalls apples blown down by the wind from trees.

Chapter 4

Summary

As summer ends and news of the rebellion spreads to other farms (by way of pigeons released by Snowball and Napoleon), Jones spends most of his time in a pub, complaining about his troubles to two neighboring farmers: Pilkington and Frederick.

In October, Jones and a group of men arrive at Animal Farm and attempt to seize control if it. Snowball turns out to be an extraordinary tactician and, with the help of the other animals, drives Jones and his men away. The animals then celebrate their victory in what they call "The Battle of the Cowshed."

Commentary

Snowball and Napoleon's decision to send pigeons to neighboring farms to spread news of Animal Farm is—like their creation of "Animal Hero, First Class" at the end of the chapter—an attempt to heighten the gravity and scope of the rebellion. By informing other animals about Animal Farm, the pigs hope to instigate rebellions elsewhere and eventually live in the world depicted in old Major's dream.

The scene of Jones commiserating in the Red Lion with Pilkington and Frederick portrays the humans as exactly the greedy self-centered beings that the animals wished to overthrow. Although the two neighboring farmers sympathize with Jones "in principle," Orwell states that each is "secretly wondering whether he could somehow turn Jones' misfortune to his own advantage." Note also that Pilkington's farm, Foxwood, is in a "disgraceful condition" and that Frederick is "perpetually involved in lawsuits" and has a "name for driving hard bargains." In direct contrast to the principles of Animalism, the humans live by a credo of self-interest and desire for material gain. (Of course, the reader has already seen how Napoleon is betraying the principles of Animalism, as he becomes more and more like these men in the pub.)

According to Frederick and Pilkington, the animals are "rebelling against the laws of nature," with "nature" in this context referring to a world where humans control all aspects of animals' lives and use them for their own material gain. Of course, what seems "natural" to the humans is not what seems "natural" to the animals, and it is worth noting that all attempts in the novel to change the natures of both humans *and* animals fail.

Driven by fear and their perception that other animals at neighboring farms are beginning to become inspired by the rebels' example, Jones attempts to take back what is his—but his attempt at military prowess in this case only further depicts him as impotent and inept. After being muted upon by the pigeons, Jones is knocked into a dung heap—a fitting place for him, in the eyes of his animal enemies. His running from the farm concludes a scene obviously serious for the characters but—with its panic and application of Caesarian tactics to a barnyard melee—comic to the reader.

Literary Device

Boxer's teary-eyed concern over the possible death of the stable-lad reinforces his simple-mindedness and foreshadows the fact that he will be unable to survive in a place as harsh as Animal Farm is soon to become. The image of the great horse trying to turn the boy over with his hoof while he laments, "Who will not believe that I did not do this on purpose?" contrasts the one of Snowball, with the blood dripping from his wounds, stating, "War is war. The only good human being is a dead one." Unlike Boxer, who wishes no real harm even to his enemies, Snowball cares little for the possible regrets one of his soldiers may face. To him, death is an inevitable by-product of revolution, as he remarks during his funeral oration for the dead sheep.

The chapter ends with the implication that Animal Farm is becoming a place grounded more in military might than agrarian industry. The creation of military decorations, the naming of the battle, and the decision to fire Jones' gun twice a year all suggest the animals' love of ceremony and the slow but sure transformation of Animal Farm into a place governed by martial law more than the Seven Commandments of Animalism.

Chapter 5

Summary

Winter comes, and Mollie works less and less. Eventually, Clover discovers that Mollie is being bribed off Animal Farm by one of Pilkington's men, who eventually wins her loyalties. Mollie disappears, and the pigeons report seeing her standing outside a pub, sporting one of the ribbons that she always coveted.

The pigs increase their influence on the farm, deciding all questions of policy and then offering their decisions to the animals, who must ratify them by a majority vote. Snowball and Napoleon continue their fervent debates, the greatest of which occurs over the building of a windmill on a knoll. Snowball argues in favor of the windmill, which he is certain will eventually become a labor-saving device; Napoleon argues against it, saying that building the windmill will take time and effort away from the more important task of producing food. The two also disagree on whether they should (as Napoleon thinks) amass an armory of guns or (as Snowball thinks) send out more pigeons to neighboring farms to spread news of the rebellion. On the Sunday that the plan for the windmill is to be put to a vote, Napoleon calls out nine ferocious dogs, who chase Snowball off the farm. Napoleon then announces that all debates will stop and institutes a number of other new rules for the farm.

Three weeks after Snowball's escape, Napoleon surprises everybody by announcing that the windmill will be built. He sends Squealer to the animals to explain that the windmill was really Napoleon's idea all along and that the plans for it were stolen from him by Snowball.

Commentary

The defection of Mollie marks her as an even greater materialist than she had appeared to be earlier in the novel. The fact that she is bribed away from Animal Farm with sugar and ribbons—two items that Snowball condemned as unnecessary for liberty in Chapter 2—shows her desire for luxury without making the necessary sacrifices to obtain it.

She is a defector from the politics of Animal Farm and is never mentioned by the other animals, who find her abandonment of Animalism and the rebellion shameful. Despite their implied condemnation, however, the pigeons do report that "She appeared to be enjoying herself"—much more so than the animals who remain on the farm. Mollie may be politically shallow in the eyes of her former comrades, but she *does* manage to secure herself a much more comfortable life, which raises the question of whether one is better off living well with one's enemies or suffering with one's comrades. The novel eventually suggests that Mollie did, in fact, make a wise decision in leaving Animal Farm, although (to be fair) she did not do so because of any political or moral motives.

At this point, the pigs have gained more power: Earlier, they were "supervisors," but now they decide "all questions of farm policy." While these decisions still need to be ratified by the other animals, Orwell suggests that the pigs are gaining ground at a slow but steady rate. But with the "bitterly hard weather" that arrives that winter, so do "bitterly hard" debates increase between Snowball and Napoleon. Actually, "debate" is hardly the correct term, since only Snowball attempts to use rhetoric and logic to sway the other animals—Napoleon uses a number of what Squealer will later call "tactics" to get his way. For example, Napoleon spends time during the week training the sheep to break into their "Four legs good, two legs bad" bleating during "crucial moments" in Snowball's speeches; packing the meetings with his own unwitting supporters is Napoleon's calculated strategy here. His unleashing of the nine dogs later in the chapter is Napoleon's ultimate "debating technique": Violence, not oratory, is how Napoleon settles disagreements.

Literary Device

The windmill itself is a symbol of technological progress. Snowball wants it to be built because he thinks it will bring to the farm a degree of self-sufficiency—which accords with the principles of Animalism. Napoleon, however, cares nothing for the windmill (and even urinates on Snowball's plans for it) because he is only concerned with establishing his totalitarian rule. At the debate on the windmill, Snowball argues that after it is built, the animals will only need to work three days a week, while Napoleon argues that "if they wasted time on the windmill they would all starve to death."

Thus, Snowball is a leader who looks forward and considers the future of his nation, while Napoleon thinks only of the present, since his vision of the future is one in which he is in full control over animals who have no time for leisure activities. (This is again emphasized when Snowball argues for spreading news of the rebellion so that *eventually* all animals will rise against oppression, while Napoleon wants to create a stockpile of weapons that he can then turn, if needed, on his own citizens.) In short, Snowball's vision of life with the windmill is like Moses' Sugarcandy Mountain: An immensely desirable yet fantastic place.

Note that Benjamin does not endorse either pig, and their slogans have no effect on him. Like the reader, he is doubtful of Snowball's scheme and wary of Napoleon's maneuvers. All Benjamin believes is what he knows for sure, the sum total of which is that, "Windmill or no windmill, life will go on as it always had gone on—that is, badly." This cynical remark is perhaps the most important statement in the entire novel, for despite all of the ideologies, plans, battles, schemes, debates, betrayals, sound, and fury of the animals, the end result is that they return full circle to the exact same life they tried to avoid. As he does several times throughout the novel, Orwell speaks directly to the reader through Benjamin.

Napoleon's newfound power is based wholly on the threat of violence, as demonstrated in his "winning" the debate with Snowball by driving him off the farm. His decision to end all debates reflects his insatiable need for power: Debates, when conducted in the spirit of inquiry and discovery of viewpoints, are crucial to a government that wants its citizens to take part in their own rule. Napoleon, however, views debates as "unnecessary" because he will permit no questioning of his command and wants to silence any dissention. Like Big Brother, the personification of the all-powerful government in Orwell's *Nineteen Eighty-Four*, Napoleon begins to become an unapproachable, godlike figure. Note that when the four porkers object to the way in which Napoleon seizes power, the dogs begin to growl, and the sheep bleat their "Four legs good" slogan over and over. This combination of relentless propaganda and threats of violence comprise Napoleon's philosophy of leadership—the same philosophy behind the government in *Nineteen Eighty-Four*. Napoleon's disinterment of Major's skull is his way of allying himself with the beloved father of Animalism—another piece of admittedly brilliant propaganda.

Theme

Squealer displays even more of his skill at doubletalk in this chapter. As he did previously with the milk and apples, Squealer paints Napoleon's crimes in a light that makes Napoleon more like a martyr than a dictator. Calling Napoleon's takeover a "sacrifice" and stating that leadership is "not a pleasure," the officious pig manages to—as was said earlier about him—"turn black into white." Even more invidious is Squealer's ability to rewrite history: He tells the animals that Snowball's part in the Battle of the Cowshed was "much exaggerated" and (once Napoleon decides to proceed with the building of the windmill) that the idea for it was Napoleon's all along. Again, as in *Nineteen Eighty-Four*, Orwell attacks the ways in which those who rise to power revise the past in order to keep their grip on the present and future. These "tactics," as Squealer calls them, allow Napoleon to always present himself in the most favorable light—and, if an animal *still* objects, the three dogs accompanying Squealer serve as ample deterrent. Faced with Squealer's "skipping" words and the mouths of the dogs, an animal has hardly a choice but to submit to the new regime.

Glossary

publican   a saloonkeeper; innkeeper.

harrows   frames with spikes or sharp-edged disks, drawn by a horse or tractor and used for breaking up and leveling plowed ground, covering seeds, rooting up weeds, etc.

binders   machines that both reap and bind grain.

Chapter 6

Summary

During the following year, the animals work harder than ever before. Building the windmill is a laborious business, and Boxer proves himself a model of physical strength and dedication. Napoleon announces that Animal Farm will begin trading with neighboring farms and hires Mr. Whymper, a solicitor, to act as his agent. Other humans meet in pubs and discuss their theories that the windmill will collapse and that Animal Farm will go bankrupt. Jones gives up his attempts at retaking his farm and moves to another part of the county. The pigs move into the farmhouse and begin sleeping in beds, which Squealer excuses on the grounds that the pigs need their rest after the daily strain of running the farm.

That November, a storm topples the half-finished windmill. Napoleon tells the animals that Snowball is responsible for its ruin and offers a reward to any animal who kills Snowball or brings him back alive. Napoleon then declares that they will begin rebuilding the windmill that very morning.

Commentary

With the passing of a year, all of the animals (save Benjamin) have wholly swallowed Napoleon's propaganda: Despite their working like "slaves," the animals believe that "everything they did was for the benefit of themselves" and "not for a pack of idle, thieving human beings." When Napoleon orders that animals will need to work on Sundays, he calls the work "strictly voluntary" yet adds that any animal who does *not* volunteer will have his rations reduced. Thus, Napoleon is able to foster a sense of unity (where animals "volunteer") using the threat of hunger. This transformation of obvious dictatorial practices (forced labor) into seemingly benevolent social programs (volunteering) is another of Napoleon's methods for keeping the animals working and docile.

The effect of Napoleon's propaganda is also seen in Boxer's unflagging devotion to the windmill. Even when warned by Clover about exerting himself, Boxer can only think, "I will work harder" and "Napoleon is always right." The fact that he can only think in slogans reflects his inability to engage in any real thought at all. Slogans such as these are powerful weapons for leaders like Napoleon, who want to keep their followers devoted, docile, and dumb.

Style & Language

One of the most effective ways that Napoleon strengthens his rule is his use of the politics of sacrifice. Indeed, "sacrifice" is an often-repeated word in the novel, and Napoleon uses it to excuse what he knows others will see as his blatant disregard for the Seven Commandments of Animalism. For example, when ordering that Animal Farm will engage in trade with human beings and that the hens must sell their eggs, he states that the hens "should welcome this sacrifice as their own special contribution towards the building of the windmill." After facing some objections from the animals about trading with humans, Napoleon tells them that they will not have to come into contact with any human beings, since, "He intended to take the whole burden upon his own shoulders." Like the apples and milk (which the pigs' pretended not to like in the first place), Napoleon masterfully recasts himself as an animal like Boxer—when, of course, the reader sees that the pig and the horse are complete opposites in their selfishness and selflessness. Of course, if any animals ever hint at seeing through Napoleon's false humility, they will be greeted with the same combination of bleating and growls that faced Snowball in Chapter 5.

Squealer continues his work of mollifying the animals who object to Napoleon's plans. As he *figuratively* rewrites history when explaining that there never was a resolution against using money or trading and that the animals must have dreamed it, he *literally* rewrites history when he changes the Fourth Commandment from "No animal shall sleep in a bed" to "No animal shall sleep in a bed with sheets." When Clover learns of the two added words, she is naturally suspicious but has been so brainwashed by Napoleon's regime that she concludes that she was mistaken. Squealer's explanation of why the pigs sleep in beds hinges on semantics rather than common sense: "A bed merely means a place to sleep in" and "A pile of straw is a bed, properly regarded" are examples of his manipulation of language. His most powerful word, of course, is "Jones," for whenever he asks, "Surely, none of you wishes to see Jones back?" all the animals' questions are dispelled.

The destruction of the windmill marks the failure of Snowball's vision of the future. It also allows Orwell to again demonstrate Napoleon's incredible ability to seize an opportunity for his own purposes. Afraid of seeming indecisive and a failure while all the animals stare at the toppled windmill, Napoleon invokes the name of Snowball as Squealer does with Jones: "Do you know," he asks, "the enemy who has come in the night and overthrown our windmill? SNOWBALL!" For the remainder of the novel, Snowball will be used as a scapegoat for all of Napoleon's failings; his commands to begin rebuilding the windmill and shouting of slogans occur because he does not want to give the animals any time in which to consider the plausibility of his story about Snowball. Although he shouts, "Long live Animal Farm," he means, "Long live Napoleon!"

Chapter 7

Summary

As the human world watches Animal Farm and waits for news of its failure, the animals struggle against starvation. Napoleon uses Mr. Whymper to spread news of Animal Farm's sufficiency to the human world. After learning that they must surrender their eggs, the hens stage a demonstration that only ends when they can no longer live without the rations that Napoleon had denied them. Nine hens die as a result of the protest.

The animals are led to believe that Snowball is visiting the farm at night and spitefully subverting their labor. He becomes a constant (and imagined) threat to the animals' security, and Squealer eventually tells the animals that Snowball has sold himself to Frederick and that he was in league with Jones from the very beginning.

One day in spring, Napoleon calls a meeting of all the animals, during which he forces confessions from all those who had questioned him (such as the four pigs in Chapters 5 and 6 and the three hens who lead the protest) and then has them murdered by the dogs. Numerous animals also confess to crimes that they claim were instigated by Snowball. Eventually, the singing of "Beasts of England" is outlawed and a new song by Minimus, Napoleon's pig-poet, is instituted, although the animals do not find the song as meaningful as their previous anthem.

Commentary

Faced with the realities of farming—and his own lack of planning for the winter—Napoleon is forced to deal with a hungry populace and the potentially damaging leaks of such news to the outside world. To surmount these problems, Napoleon metaphorically assumes the role of director and mounts a theatrical production. In terms of this metaphor, Mr. Whymper is the audience whom Napoleon must engage and fool into believing in an illusion, the sheep are actors reciting lines about the rations having been increased, and the empty grain bins filled with sand are the props (or "special effects"). Whymper is fooled into thinking that Animal Farm is running smoothly, and Napoleon again demonstrates his judicious use of deception. (Ironically, this deceptive theatricality is exactly what Squealer later accuses Snowball of having done with Jones at the Battle of the Cowshed.)

More deception occurs in the pernicious lies spread about Snowball. Napoleon uses him as a scapegoat for any of the farm's misfortunes, as Hitler did with European Jews as he rose to power. Both leaders understand the public's desire to cast blame on an outside source for all their troubles. Squealer's claims that the pigs have found "documents" linking Snowball to Jones are an appeal to the animals' need for proof—although the nonexistent documents are never revealed to them on the grounds that the animals are unable to read them. Like the grain-bins filled with sand, Snowball's "documents" are another ruse used by Napoleon to manipulate the thoughts of those who could end his rule. The animals refuse to believe that the thin walls of the windmill contributed to its collapse, revealing the extent to which they subscribe to the Snowball-baiting ideology.

Those who actually *do* threaten Napoleon's rule are dealt with in a swift and brutal fashion. Napoleon calls a meeting of all the animals for the purpose of publicly executing dissidents in order to make the others understand what will happen to them should they refuse one of his orders. When the four pigs who protested against Napoleon's decision to end the Sunday meetings are called before him, they confess to have been secretly in touch with Snowball, in the hopes of receiving some clemency from Napoleon. This is the same technique used by the hens, who, likewise, are slaughtered. The number of other animals who confess to Snowball-inspired crimes, however, suggests the degree to which paranoia has gripped the animals, who now feel the need to confess things as slight as stealing six ears of corn or urinating in the drinking water. The scene of these confessions echoes the Salem witch trials, where seemingly rational people suddenly confessed to having comported with Satan as a way of relieving their psychological torments. Afraid that their crimes will be discovered, the animals confess them because they are unable to stand the strain of their guilt.

The terrible atmosphere of fear and death that now characterizes Animal Farm is discussed by Boxer and Clover at the end of the chapter. Boxer, naturally, concludes that he must work harder to atone for "some fault in ourselves"; like the confessing animals, he wants to purge himself of nonexistent evils. Clover, however, does gain a small amount of insight as she looks at the farm from the knoll and considers that the terrors she has seen were not in her mind when old Major spoke of his dream. However, since she lacked "the words to express" these ideas, her possibly revolutionary thoughts are never brought out. With Snowball gone, none of the animals are encouraged to read—for the same reasons that slaves throughout history were similarly deprived.

Napoleon's outlawing "Beasts of England" is his next step in assuming total control. Fearful that the song might stir up the same rebellious feelings felt by the animals the night Major taught it to them, Napoleon replaces it with a decidedly blander song that focuses on the responsibility of the animals to protect the farm, rather than to overthrow its leaders:

> Animal Farm, Animal Farm,
>
> Never through me shalt thou come to harm!

Of course, there is no debate about this decision, since the sheep who accompany Squealer effectively end all talk of it with their incessant bleating. Nothing at Animal Farm will ever be the same since the blood of animals has been shed by their own kind.

Glossary

clamps piles of straw or peat under which potatoes are grown.

chaff the husks of wheat or other grain separated in threshing or winnowing.

Chapter 8

Summary

The following year brings more work on the windmill and less food for the workers, despite Squealer's lists of figures supposedly proving that food production has increased dramatically under Napoleon's rule. As Napoleon grows more powerful, he is seen in public less often. The general opinion of him is expressed in a poem by Minimus that lists his merits and virtues. More executions occur while Napoleon schemes to sell a pile of timber to Frederick—who is alternately rumored to be a sadistic torturer of animals and the victim of unfounded gossip.

After the completion of the new windmill in August, Napoleon sells the pile of timber to Frederick, who tries to pay with a check. Napoleon, however, demands cash, which he receives. Whymper then learns that Frederick's banknotes are forgeries, and Napoleon pronounces the death sentence on the traitorous human.

The next morning, Frederick and 14 men arrive at Animal Farm and attempt to take it by force. Although the humans are initially successful, after they blow up the windmill, the animals are completely enraged and drive the men from the farm. Squealer explains to the bleeding animals that, despite what they may think, they were actually victorious in what will hereafter be called "The Battle of the Windmill."

Some days later, the pigs discover a case of whisky in Jones' cellar. After drinking too much of it, Napoleon fears he is dying and decrees that the drinking of alcohol is punishable by death. Two days later, however, Napoleon feels better and orders the small paddock (which was to have been used as a retirement-home for old animals) to be ploughed and planted with barley. The chapter ends with Muriel rereading the Seven Commandments and noticing, for the first time, that the Fifth Commandment now reads, "No animal shall drink alcohol to excess."

Commentary

The number of executions occurring at the farm naturally raises some concerns among the animals, who recall the Sixth Commandment of Animalism: "No animal shall kill any other animal." However, as he has done many times already, Napoleon revises the past to suit his present aims and alters the painted Commandment to read, "No animal shall kill any other animal without cause." The addition of two words gives Napoleon free rein to kill whomever he wishes (since *he* determines all "causes"), and these two words echo the other additions to the commandments: "with sheets" to the Fourth and "to excess" to the Fifth. In all three cases, a minor grammatical revision permits major revision of a law that legitimizes and excuses Napoleon's tyranny.

Theme

As the work on the windmill continues, the animals *do* begin to starve, as Napoleon originally said they would in his debates with Snowball. Ever the happy sycophant, however, Squealer readily provides lists of figures to prove to the animals that they are *not* starving. Benjamin Disraeli, the former Prime Minister of England, once remarked, "There are three kinds of lies: Lies, damned lies, and statistics"—a remark that Squealer's actions here prove true. Like many people, the animals are dazzled by numbers as indicative of scientific sampling and concrete information, despite the fact that "they would have sooner had less figures and more food." Official sounding "evidence" thus convinces the animals that their own rumbling stomachs must be in the wrong.

Character Insight

Now that he is in total and undisputed control of Animal Farm, Napoleon becomes a paranoid egomaniac, and Orwell stresses this new phase of Napoleon's character in several ways. First, he virtually vanishes from public; when he *is* seen, he is first heralded by a black cockerel. Second, he lives in separate rooms from the other pigs and only eats from Jones' Crown Derby dinner service. Third, he orders the gun to be fired on his birthday and is referred to with flattering epithets, such as "Protector of the Sheep-fold." Fourth, he orders Minimus' poem about himself to be inscribed on the wall of the big barn, surmounted by a painting of his profile. Fifth, he has a pig named Pinkeye taste all of his food to be sure it is not poisoned. Sixth, he names the completed windmill Napoleon Mill and, after selling the timber, has the animals slowly walk past him as he lies on a bed of straw next to his piles of money. Again, Orwell displays a politician's image as a powerful means of controlling his subjects.

None of these unabashed displays of his own importance, however, deter the animals from worshipping him. The poem written by Minimus is notable for the ways in which it resembles a prayer, likening Napoleon to "the sun in the sky" and flattering him with lines like, "Thou are the giver of / All that thy creatures love." (Note the formal poetic diction found in words like "Thou," "Ere," and "thee" that seemingly elevates the dignity of the poem's subject.) As a whole, however, the poem portrays Napoleon as an omniscient force ("Thou watches over all, / Comrade Napoleon") that begins brainwashing his subjects from their first living moments:

> "Had I a sucking pig,
> Ere he had grown as big
> Even as a pint bottle or a rolling-pin,
> He should have learned to be
> Faithful and true to thee,
> Yes, his first squeak should be
> "Comrade Napoleon!"

Unlike "Beasts of England," which called for an uprising against tyranny and an increased sense of unity among all animals, Minimus' poem portrays Napoleon as a greater and better animal than all others, deserving their full devotion. On the surface, such a song of praise might seem like innocent flattery—but the reader understands that the poem is another weapon in Napoleon's propaganda arsenal.

Napoleon's relationship with Frederick and Pilkington also reveal his disregard for old Major's principles; indeed, Orwell remarks that relations between Napoleon and Pilkington become "almost friendly." When the animals are shocked to learn that Napoleon "had really been in secret agreement with Frederick" to sell him the timber, the reader (as with Minimus' poem) senses the truth and understands that there never was a "secret agreement," but that Napoleon had been sounding each man to see who would offer him a better price. Again Napoleon is able to manipulate the animals' perceptions in order to make himself appear in complete control. The pigeons that Napoleon releases with their varying slogans ("Death to Frederick" and "Death to Pilkington") resemble government-controlled media, spreading the official word on a topic to the world and completely contradicting all previous statements when necessary.

Another way in which Napoleon manipulates public opinion is his naming the windmill "Napoleon Mill." Building the windmill had been an effort of *all* the animals, but Napoleon names it after himself to again insinuate that Animal Farm has become what it is because of *his* actions. Ironically, this is true in both the positive and negative sense: Napoleon's leadership *has* freed the animals from human control—but it has also begun to enslave them to another form of tyranny. As Snowball is deemed responsible for everything that goes wrong on the farm, Napoleon is credited with all improvements. The animals praising him for the taste of the water and other things with which Napoleon obviously had nothing to do reveals the depth to which he has pervaded their minds—and terrified them into complete dependence and obedience.

Literary Device

The destruction of the windmill marks Animal Farm's final, irrevocable turn for the worse. As the windmill earlier symbolized the hopes of Snowball and a future of leisure, its explosion at the hands of Frederick symbolizes the absolute impossibility of Snowball's dreams. The Battle of the Windmill recalls, of course, the Battle of the Cowshed, but this battle is more chaotic, more bloody, and less effective than the former: "A cow, three sheep, and two geese were killed, and nearly everyone was wounded."

Literary Device

Like the statistics that "proved" that the animals could not be hungry, Squealer's logic in proving that the battle was a victory is an incredible display of political doubletalk at its most obvious and ludicrous: Boxer, bleeding and wounded, cannot conceive how Squealer can call the battle a victory, until the pig explains, "The enemy was in occupation of this very ground that we stand upon. And now—thanks to the leadership of comrade Napoleon—we have won every inch of it back again!" Boxer's deadpan reply to this—"Then we have won back what we had before"—contains a wisdom that even he cannot appreciate, for he is attempting to follow Squealer's logic while simultaneously (and unknowingly) pointing out the laughable nature of Squealer's claim. Here, as elsewhere, the satire of *Animal Farm* grows exponentially sharper and more bitter with each chapter.

The episode involving the alcohol is notable for the way in which it further characterizes the pigs as the gluttonous animals they are thought to be in the popular imagination, as well as how it offers another example of Napoleon's cold efficiency: His decision to use that paddock as a place to harvest barley instead of the old-age home it was originally earmarked to be clearly indicates that Napoleon values profits (and homemade spirits) over revering the aged.

Chapter 9

Summary

After celebrating their so-called victory against Frederick, the animals begin building a new windmill. Their efforts are again led by Boxer who, despite his split hoof, insists on working harder and getting the windmill started before he retires.

Food supplies continue to diminish, but Squealer explains that they actually have more food and better lives than they have ever known. The four sows litter 31 piglets; Napoleon, the father of all of them, orders a schoolroom to be built for their education. Meanwhile, more and more of the animals' rations are reduced while the pigs continue to grow fatter. Animal Farm is eventually proclaimed a Republic, and Napoleon is elected President.

Once his hoof heals, Boxer works as hard as he can at building the windmill—until the day he collapses because of a lung ailment. After he is helped back to his stall, Squealer informs them that Napoleon has sent for the veterinarian at Willingdon to treat him. When the van arrives to take Boxer to the hospital, however, Benjamin reads its side and learns that Boxer is actually being taken to a knacker, or glue-boiler. Clover screams to Boxer to escape, but the old horse is too weak to kick his way out of the van, which drives away. Boxer is never seen again. To placate the animals, Squealer tells them that Boxer was not taken to a knacker but that the veterinarian had bought the knacker's truck and had not yet repainted the words on its side. The animals are relieved when they hear this. The chapter ends with a grocer's van delivering a crate of whisky to the pigs, who drink it all and do not arise until after noon the following day.

Commentary

Character Insight

Boxer's death in this chapter marks him as the most pathetic of Orwell's creations. Completely brainwashed by Napoleon, he lives (and dies) for the good of the farm—a farm whose leader sells him to a knacker the moment he becomes unfit for work. His naiveté in looking forward to his retirement and pension fulfills the promise of the white line down his face, which Orwell tells the reader in Chapter 1 gives him a "somewhat stupid appearance." Even when stricken and unable to move, Boxer can only consider what his ailment will mean to the windmill, and his pipe dream of retiring with Benjamin and learning "the remaining twenty-two letters of the alphabet" is as far-flung as Snowball's utopia and Moses' Sugarcandy Mountain.

Theme

The scene in which Boxer is taken to his death is notable for its depiction of a powerless and innocent figure caught in the gears of unforgiving tyranny. (Note that the van's driver wears a bowler hat—a symbol throughout the novel of cruel humanity.) Although Boxer tries to kick his way out of the van, his previously incredible strength has been—through days of mindless hard work in the service of his tormentors—reduced to nothing. Only in his last moments does Boxer begin to understand what is happening to him, but the knowledge comes too late for anything to change.

Theme

This chapter also continues to display Squealer's manipulation of language for the pigs' political ends. In his famous essay, "Politics and the English Language" (1946), Orwell discusses the many ways that our language "becomes ugly and inaccurate because our thoughts are foolish," but also argues that "the slovenliness of our language makes it easier to have foolish thoughts." In other words, any corruption of the language can (and will) have a corrupting influence on the ways in which we think about the very things that language struggles to describe. This process is illustrated in Squealer's announcements to the animals about their shortages of food: "For the time being," he explains, "it had been found necessary to make a readjustment of rations." His use of "readjustment" instead of "reduction" is a subtle attempt to quell the animals' complaints about their stomachs—"reduction" is a word implying *less* of something, but "readjustment" implies a *shifting* of what is already there. (Thus one hears politicians speak of "the need to increase funding of government programs" instead of "tax hikes" or the invasion of another country as a "police action" instead of a "war.") In "Politics and the English Language," Orwell contends that such euphemisms are used because they prevent listeners from conjuring mental pictures of what is being described, which in turn lessens the amount of horror listeners can feel when considering the topic.

This manipulation of language is again found when Animal Farm is proclaimed a Republic, with Napoleon its "elected" President. The word "Republic" connotes a land of self-government whose citizens participate in the political process, as the word "President" connotes one who is *of* the citizenry but who has been appointed by them to preside over—not control—their government. Of course, these words are outrageous jokes to the reader, but not to the animals, who again and again swallow the pigs' twisted language to make themselves feel better: As Orwell slyly remarks, "Doubtless it had been worse in the old days. They were glad to believe so."

Similarly, the animals are "glad to believe" Squealer's obvious lies about Boxer's final moments in which he supposedly praised both Animals Farm and Napoleon. This is Squealer's most outrageous and blatant piece of propaganda, and a reader may well wonder why none of the animals raise the slightest suspicion about it. The reason is that they are afraid to do so—afraid of Napoleon and his dogs, of course, but also afraid of probing too deeply into the story and thus upsetting their own consciences. Believing Squealer is easier politically and morally. They can excuse their lack of action by willingly believing Squealer's lies about the owner of the van. As Orwell ironically explains:

> The animals were enormously relieved to hear this. And when Squealer went on to give further graphic details of Boxer's death-bed, the admirable care he had received, and the expensive medicines for which Napoleon had paid without a thought to the cost, their last doubts disappeared and the sorrow that they felt for their comrade's death was tempered by the thought that at least he had died happy.

Words like "admirable," "expensive," and "without a thought to the cost" all give the animals license to excuse their own inaction. As Orwell wrote elsewhere, "To see what is in front of one's nose needs a constant struggle"—a struggle that the animals doubtless are able to overcome.

The return of Moses is, like the destruction of the first windmill, used to the pigs' advantage. A reader may wonder why the pigs allow Moses to remain on the farm (and actually encourage him to do so by giving him a gill of beer a day). The reason lies in the effect Moses has on the animals. Again recalling Marx's famous metaphor, Moses' tales of Sugarcandy Mountain figuratively drug the animals and keep them docile: If life now is awful, at least (so Moses' tales imply) it will not always be such. Therefore the animals continue working, laboring under the hope that, one day, Moses' stories will come true.

Napoleon's fathering of the 31 piglets suggests how saturated with his image and presence the farm has become. In a biological sense, Napoleon is now creating the very population he means to control. His decision to build a schoolhouse for the pigs is reminiscent of such fascist organizations as the Hitler Youth, and his numerous decrees favoring the pigs (such as the one requiring all animals to step out of their way when approached by pigs) recalls Hitler's thoughts about Aryan superiority.

Also notable in this chapter is the great amount of ceremony that Napoleon institutes throughout the farm: The increased amount of songs, speeches, and demonstrations keep the animals' brains busy enough not to think about their own wretchedness—and Napoleon packs the meetings with the sheep in case any animals momentarily see past all the pomp and circumstance. The wreath Napoleon orders to be made for Boxer's grave is a similar display for Napoleon's own ends, as is the elegy for Boxer that he ends with the horse's two maxims in order to threaten the other animals. The fact that the pigs get drunk on the night of the supposed solemn day of Boxer's memorial banquet betrays their complete lack of sympathy for the devoted but ignorant horse. Their drunkenness also makes them more like Jones, their former oppressor.

Glossary

gill   a unit of liquid measure, equal to ¼ pint or 4 fluid ounces.

Chapter 10

Summary

Years pass, and Animal Farm undergoes its final changes. Muriel, Bluebell, Jessie, and Pincher are all dead, and Jones dies in an inebriates' home. Clover is now 14 years old (two years past the retiring age) but has not retired. (No animal ever has.) There are more animals on the farm, and the farm's boundaries have increased, thanks to the purchase of two of Pilkington's fields. The second windmill has been completed and is used for milling corn. All the animals continue their lives of hard work and little food—except, of course, for the pigs.

One evening, Clover sees a shocking sight: Squealer walking on his hind legs. Other pigs follow, walking the same way, and Napoleon also emerges from the farmhouse carrying a whip in his trotter. The sheep begin to bleat a new version of their previous slogan: "Four legs good, two legs better!" Clover also notices that the wall on which the Seven Commandments were written has been repainted: Now, the wall simply reads, "ALL ANIMALS ARE EQUAL / BUT SOME ANIMALS ARE MORE EQUAL THAN OTHERS." Eventually, all the pigs begin carrying whips and wearing Jones' clothes.

In the novel's final scene, a deputation of neighboring farmers are given a tour of the farm, after which they meet in the dining-room of the farmhouse with Napoleon and the other pigs. Mr. Pilkington makes a toast to Animal Farm and its efficiency. Napoleon then offers a speech in which he outlines his new policies: The word "comrade" will be suppressed, there will be no more Sunday meetings, the skull of old Major has been buried, and the farm flag will be changed to a simple field of green. His greatest change in policy, however, is his announcement that Animal Farm will again be called Manor Farm. Soon after Napoleon's speech, the men and pigs begin playing cards, but a loud quarrel erupts when both Napoleon and Pilkington each try to play the ace of spades. As Clover and the other animals watch the arguments through the dining-room window, they are unable to discriminate between the humans and the pigs.

Commentary

This final chapter depicts the complete transformation (not only in name) from Animal Farm to Manor Farm. There will never be a "retirement home" for old animals (as evidenced by Clover), and the pigs come to resemble their human oppressors to the degree that "it was impossible to say which was which."

The completion of the second windmill marks not the rebirth of Snowball's utopian vision, but a further linking of the animals and humans: Used not for a dynamo but instead for milling corn (and thus making money), the windmill's symbolic meaning has (like everything else) been reversed and corrupted. Animal Farm is now inexorably tied to its human neighbors in terms of commerce and atmosphere.

Theme

Orwell has years pass between Chapters 9 and 10 to stress the ways in which the animals' lack of any sense of history has rendered them incapable of judging their present situation: The animals cannot complain about their awful lives, since "they had nothing to go upon except Squealer's lists of figures, which invariably demonstrated that everything was getting better and better." As Winston Smith, the protagonist of Orwell's *Nineteen-Eight-Four* understands, the government "could thrust its hand into the past and say of this or that event *it never happened.*" This same phenomena occurs now on Animal Farm, where the animals cannot recall there ever having been a way of life different from their present one and, therefore, no way of life to which they can compare their own. Although "Beasts of England" is hummed in secret by some would-be rebels, "no one dared to sing it aloud." The pigs have won their ideological battle, as the Party wins its war with Winston's mind at the end of *Nineteen-Eight-Four.* Only Benjamin—a means by which Orwell again voices his own opinion of the matter—is able to conclude that "hunger, hardship, and disappointment" are the "unalterable law of life."

While Clover is shocked at the sight of Squealer walking on two legs, the reader is not, since this moment is the logical result of all the pigs' previous machinations. Napoleon's carrying a whip in his trotter—formerly a symbol of human torture—and dressing in Jones' clothes only cements in readers minds what they have long suspected. The sheep's new slogan, as before, destroys any chance for thought or debate on the animals' part, and the new Commandment painted on the wall perfectly (and ironically) expresses Napoleon's philosophy. Of course, the phrase "more equal" is paradoxical, but this illustrates the paradoxical notion of animals oppressing their own kind *in the name of* liberty and unity. When the deputation of neighboring humans arrives, the animals are not sure whom they should fear: The pigs or the men. Orwell implies here that there is no real difference, as he does with the pigs buying a wireless, a telephone, and newspapers, and with Napoleon smoking a pipe, despite old Major's admonition to avoid all habits of men.

Pilkington's address to Napoleon is sniveling in tone and reveals his desire to remain on good terms with the intimidating leader of Animal Farm. Excusing all cruelty and apologizing for being "nervous" about the effects of the rebellion, Pilkington offers a stream of empty words said only to keep the wheels of commerce well-greased. Note that he *praises* Napoleon for making the animals do more work for less food; flattery from such a man can only suggest that the object of such praise is as corrupt as he who flatters. His final witticism—"If you have your lower animals to contend with . . . we have our lower classes!"—again stresses the political interchangeability between the pigs and the men.

The changes of which Napoleon speaks in his address are the final ones needed to make the farm a complete dictatorship. The abolition of the word "comrade" will create less unity among the animals, the burial of old Major's skull will figuratively "bury" any notions of the dead pig's ideals, and the removal of the horn and hoof from the flag will ensure that the animals over which it waves never consider the rewards of struggle and rebellion. Finally, the changing of the farm's name back to Manor Farm implies that everything has come full circle while also implying that the farm is not, in any sense, the animals'. Instead, it is the property of those (as Hamlet quips in Shakespeare's play) "to the manor born": the pigs.

The novel's final scene in which Napoleon and Pilkington argue about two aces of spades brilliantly represents the entire book: After years of oppression, struggle, rebellion, and reform, the pigs have become as corrupt and cruel as their masters. Smoking, drinking, whipping, killing, and even cheating are now qualities shared by both animal and man. Despite Pilkington's professed admiration for Napoleon (and vice versa), neither trusts the other because neither can: Each is motivated purely by self-interest and not the altruistic yet ineffectual principles once expounded by old Major.

Glossary

wireless set   a radio.

John Bull, Tit-Bits and The Daily Mirror   British periodicals.

CHARACTER ANALYSES

The following critical analyses delve into the physical, emotional, and psychological traits of the literary work's major characters so that you might better understand what motivates these characters. The writer of this study guide provides this scholarship as an educational tool by which you may compare your own interpretations of the characters. Before reading the character analyses that follow, consider first writing your own short essays on the characters as an exercise by which you can test your understanding of the original literary work. Then, compare your essays to those that follow, noting discrepancies between the two. If your essays appear lacking, that might indicate that you need to re-read the original literary work or re-familiarize yourself with the major characters.

Old Major

A wise and persuasive pig, old Major inspires the rebellion with his rhetorical skill and ability to get the other animals to share his indignation. When he announces that he wishes to share the contents of his strange dream with his companions, all the animals comply, demonstrating the great respect they have for such an important (that is, "major") figure. His speech about the tyranny of man is notable for its methodical enumeration of man's wrongs against the animals. Listing all of man's crimes, old Major rouses the other animals into planning the rebellion. His leading them in singing "Beasts of England" is another demonstration of his rhetorical skills, for after he teaches the animals the song about a world untainted by human hands, the animals sing it five times in succession.

The flaw in old Major's thinking is that he places *total* blame on man for *all* the animals' ills. According to him, once they "Remove Man from the scene," then "the root cause of hunger and overwork" will be abolished forever. Clearly, old Major believes that Man is capable only of doing harm and that animals are capable only of doing good. Such one-dimensional thinking that ignores the desire for power inherent in *all* living things can only result in its being disproved. Also ironic is old Major's admonition to the animals: "Remember also that in fighting against Man, we must not come to resemble him." This warning is ignored by Napoleon and the other pigs, who, by the novel's end, completely resemble their human masters.

Snowball

Snowball is the animal most clearly attuned to old Major's thinking, and he devotes himself to bettering the animals in intellectual, moral, and physical ways. He brings literacy to the farm so that the animals can better grasp the principles of Animalism by reading the Seven Commandments he paints on the barn wall. He also reduces the Commandments to a single precept ("Four legs good, two legs bad") so that even the least intelligent animals can understand the farm's new philosophy. The "thinker" of the rebellion, Snowball shows a great understanding of strategy during the Battle of the Cowshed, and while his various committees may fail, the fact that he attempts to form them reveals the degree to which he wants to better the animals' lives. His plan for the windmill is similarly noble, since its construction would give the animals more leisure time. His expulsion at the hands of Napoleon, however, suggests that force—not good intentions—governs the farm.

Napoleon

While Jones' tyranny can be somewhat excused due to the fact that he is a dull-witted drunkard, Napoleon's can only be ascribed to his blatant lust for power. The very first description of Napoleon presents him as a "fierce-looking" boar "with a reputation for getting his own way." Throughout the novel, Napoleon's method of "getting his own way" involves a combination of propaganda and terror that none of the animals can resist. Note that as soon as the revolution is won, Napoleon's first action is to steal the cows' milk for the pigs. Clearly, the words of old Major inspired Napoleon not to fight against tyranny, but to seize the opportunity to establish himself as a dictator. The many crimes he commits against his own comrades range from seizing nine puppies to "educate" them as his band of killer guard dogs to forcing confessions from innocent animals and then having them killed before all the animals' eyes.

Napoleon's greatest crime, however, is his complete transformation into Jones—although Napoleon is a much more harsh and stern master than the reader is led to believe Jones ever was. By the end of the novel, Napoleon is sleeping in Jones' bed, eating from Jones' plate, drinking alcohol, wearing a derby hat, walking on two legs, trading with humans, and sharing a toast with Mr. Pilkington. His final act of propaganda— changing the Seventh Commandment to "ALL ANIMALS ARE EQUAL / BUT SOME ARE MORE EQUAL THAN OTHERS"— reflects his unchallenged belief that he *belongs* in complete control of the farm. His restoration of the name Manor Farm shows just how much Napoleon has wholly disregarded the words of old Major.

Squealer

Every tyrant has his sycophants, and Napoleon has one in Squealer, a clever pig who (as the animals say) "could turn black into white." Throughout the novel, he serves as Napoleon's mouthpiece and Minister of Propaganda. Every time an act of Napoleon's is questioned by the other animals—regardless of how selfish or severe it may seem—Squealer is able to convince the animals that Napoleon is only acting in their best interests and that Napoleon himself has made great sacrifices for Animal Farm. For example, after Squealer is questioned about Napoleon's stealing the milk and windfallen apples, he explains that Napoleon and his fellow pigs *must* take the milk and apples because they "contain substances absolutely necessary to the well-being of a pig." He further explains that many pigs "actually dislike milk and apples" and tells the questioning animals, "It is for your sake that we drink that milk and eat those apples." His physical "skipping from side to side" during such explanations parallels his "skipping" words, which are never direct and always skirt the obvious truth of the matter at hand. As the novel proceeds, he excuses Napoleon's tyranny and sullies Snowball's reputation, just as Napoleon desires. The most outrageous demonstration of his "skipping" is when he convinces the animals that Boxer was taken to a veterinary hospital instead of the knacker's.

Boxer

Horses are universally prized for their strength, and Boxer is no exception: Standing almost six-feet tall, Boxer is a devoted citizen of the farm whose incredible strength is a great asset to the rebellion and the farm. As soon as he learns about Animalism, Boxer throws himself into the rebellion's cause. At the Battle of the Cowshed, Boxer proves to be a valuable soldier, knocking a stable-boy unconscious with his mighty hoof. (Note that Boxer, however, is not bloodthirsty and feels great remorse when he thinks he has killed the boy.) His rising early to work on the farm and his personal maxim—"I will work harder"—reveal his devotion to the animals' cause. He also proves himself to be the most valuable member of the windmill-building team.

Boxer's great strength, however, is matched by his equally stunning innocence and naiveté. He is not an intelligent animal (recall his inability to learn any of the alphabet past the letter D) and therefore can only think in simple slogans, the second of which ("Napoleon is always right") reveals his childlike dependence on an all-knowing leader. Even when he collapses while rebuilding the windmill, his first thoughts are not of himself but of the work: "It is my lung . . . It does not matter. I think you will be able to finish the windmill without me." His hopes of retiring with Benjamin after his collapse display the extent of his innocence, since the reader knows that Napoleon has no intention of providing for an old, infirm horse. Even when he is being led to his death at the knacker's, Boxer needs to be told of his terrible fate by Benjamin and Clover. He becomes wise to Napoleon's ways too late, and his death is another example of Napoleon's tyranny.

Mollie

Unlike Boxer, who always thinks of others, Mollie is a shallow materialist who cares nothing for the struggles of her fellow animals. Her first appearance in the novel suggests her personality when she enters the meeting at the last moment, chewing sugar and sitting in the front so that the others will be able to admire the red ribbons she wears in her mane. Her only concerns about the revolution are ones prompted by her ego: When she asks Snowball if they will still have sugar and ribbons after the rebellion, she betrays the thoughts of old Major and reveals her vanity. She is lulled off the farm by the prospect of more material possessions than she could enjoy in an animal-governed world, marking her as one to whom politics and struggle mean nothing.

Benjamin

As horses are known for their strength, donkeys are known for their stubbornness, and Benjamin stubbornly refuses to become enthusiastic about the rebellion. While all of his comrades delight in the prospect of a new, animal-governed world, Benjamin only remarks, "Donkeys live a long time. None of you has ever seen a dead donkey." While this reply puzzles the animals, the reader understands Benjamin's cynical yet not-unfounded point: In the initial moments of the rebellion, Animal Farm may seem a paradise, but in time it may come to be another form of the same tyranny at which they rebelled. Of course, Benjamin is proven right by the novel's end, and the only thing that he knows for sure—"Life would go on as it had always gone on—that is, badly"— proves to be a definitive remark about the animals' lives. Although pessimistic, he is a realist.

Moses

With his tales of the "promised land" to which all animals retire after death, Moses is the novel's "religious" figure. Like his biblical counterpart, Moses offers his listeners descriptions of a place—Sugarcandy Mountain—where they can live free from oppression and hunger. At first, the pigs find him irksome, since they want the animals to believe that Animal Farm is a paradise and fear that the animals will be prompted by Moses' tales to seek a better place. However, as conditions on the farm worsen, the pigs allow Moses to stay because his tales offer the animals the promise of rest after a weary, toilsome life. As Karl Marx famously stated, "Religion is the opium of the people," and Moses' tales of Sugarcandy Mountain likewise serve as an opiate to the animals' misery.

Jones

Like George III to the American colonists or Czar Nicholas II to the Russian revolutionaries, Jones is the embodiment of the tyranny against which the animals rebel—and with good reason. An inept farmer and slovenly drunkard, Jones cares little for his Manor Farm and the animals who live there. The novel's first paragraph describes Jones forgetting (out of drunkenness) to shut the popholes for the hen-houses but remembering to draw himself a glass of beer before "lumbering" off to a drunken sleep. The fact that the rebellion is sparked by Jones' forgetting to feed the animals adds to the overall impression of him as an uncaring master. For the remainder of the novel, he is portrayed as an impotent has-been, unable to reclaim his own farm and idling in a pub until his eventual death in an inebriates' home.

Long after Jones has been driven from the farm, the pigs invoke his name to scare the other animals into submission. Squealer's question, "Surely, comrades, you do not want Jones back?" elicits a knee-jerk reaction in the animals, who fail to realize that the *spirit* of Jones has returned, despite the farmer's physical absence.

Frederick

The crafty owner of Pinchfield, a neighboring farm, Frederick is "perpetually involved in lawsuits" and reveals himself to be a cutthroat businessman. Despite his offers of sympathy to Jones about the rebellion at his farm, Frederick inwardly hopes that he can "somehow turn Jones' misfortune to his own advantage." He attempts this by offering to buy a load of timber from Napoleon but paying for it with counterfeit notes. His subsequent attempt to take Animal Farm by force reveals him to be a man who always takes what he wants—in short, exactly the kind of man against which the animals initially wanted to rebel. By the novel's end, however, Napoleon has proven himself to be more greedy and double-dealing than Frederick at his worst.

Pilkington

The owner of Foxwood, a neighboring farm in "disgraceful" condition, Pilkington becomes an ally to Napoleon. This alliance, however, has a rocky start, when Napoleon changes the pigeons' message of "Death to Frederick" to "Death to Pilkington" and Pilkington refuses to help when the farm is attacked by Frederick. However, Napoleon and Pilkington eventually reconcile since they are, in essence, made of the same moral fiber and need each other to prosper (as seen when Pilkington sells part of his land to Napoleon). In the novel's last scene, Pilkington praises what Napoleon has done with Animal Farm, getting more work out of the animals with less food and likening the "lower animals" to humanity's "lower classes." The final moments of the novel, when Pilkington and Napoleon each attempt to cheat the other at cards, shows that their "friendship" is simply a facade each is using in order to better swindle the other.

CRITICAL ESSAYS

On the pages that follow, the writer of this study guide provides critical scholarship on various aspects of George Orwell's *Animal Farm*. These interpretive essays are intended solely to enhance your understanding of the original literary work; they are supplemental materials and are not to replace your reading of *Animal Farm*. When you're finished reading *Animal Farm*, and prior to your reading this study guide's critical essays, consider making a bulleted list of what you think are the most important themes and symbols. Write a short paragraph under each bullet explaining *why* you think that theme or symbol is important; include at least one short quote from the original literary work that supports your contention. Then, test your list and reasons against those found in the following essays. Do you include themes and symbols that the study guide author doesn't? If so, this self test might indicate that you are well on your way to understanding original literary work. But if not, perhaps you will need to re-read *Animal Farm*.

Animal Farm and the Russian Revolution

One of Orwell's goals in writing *Animal Farm* was to portray the Russian (or Bolshevik) Revolution of 1917 as one that resulted in a government more oppressive, totalitarian, and deadly than the one it overthrew. Many of the characters and events of Orwell's novel parallel those of the Russian Revolution: In short, Manor Farm is a model of Russia, and Old Major, Snowball, and Napoleon represent the dominant figures of the Russian Revolution.

Mr. Jones is modeled on Tsar Nicholas II (1868–1918), the last Russian emperor. His rule (1894–1917) was marked by his insistence that he was the uncontestable ruler of the nation. During his reign, the Russian people experienced terrible poverty and upheaval, marked by the Bloody Sunday massacre in 1905 when unarmed protesters demanding social reforms were shot down by the army near Nicholas' palace. As the animals under Jones lead lives of hunger and want, the lives of millions of Russians worsened during Nicholas' reign. When Russia entered World War I and subsequently lost more men than any country in any previous war, the outraged and desperate people began a series of strikes and mutinies that signaled the end of Tsarist control. When his own generals withdrew their support of him, Nicholas abdicated his throne in the hopes of avoiding an all-out civil war—but the civil war arrived in the form of the Bolshevik Revolution, when Nicholas, like Jones, was removed from his place of rule and then died shortly thereafter.

Old Major is the animal version of V. I. Lenin (1870–1924), the leader of the Bolshevik Party that seized control in the 1917 Revolution. As old Major outlines the principles of Animalism, a theory holding that all animals are equal and must revolt against their oppressors, Lenin was inspired by Karl Marx's theory of Communism, which urges the "workers of the world" to unite against their economic oppressors. As Animalism imagines a world where all animals share in the prosperity of the farm, Communism argues that a "communal" way of life will allow all people to live lives of economic equality. Old Major dies before he can see the final results of the revolution, as Lenin did before witnessing the ways in which his disciples carried on the work of reform.

Old Major is absolute in his hatred of Man, as Lenin was uncompromising in his views: He is widely believed to have been responsible for giving the order to kill Nicholas and his family after the Bolsheviks had gained control. Lenin was responsible for changing Russia into the

U.S.S.R., as old Major is responsible for transforming Manor Farm into Animal Farm. The U.S.S.R.'s flag depicted a hammer and sickle—the tools of the rebelling workers—so the flag of Animal Farm features a horn and hoof.

One of Lenin's allies was Leon Trotsky (1879–1940), another Marx-ist thinker who participated in a number of revolutionary demonstra-tions and uprisings. His counterpart in *Animal Farm* is Snowball, who, like Trotsky, felt that a worldwide series of rebellions was necessary to achieve the revolution's ultimate aims. Snowball's plans for the wind-mill and programs reflect Trotsky's intellectual character and ideas about the best ways to transform Marx's theories into practice. Trotsky was also the leader of Lenin's Red Army, as Snowball directs the army of ani-mals that repel Jones.

Eventually, Trotsky was exiled from the U.S.S.R. and killed by the agents of Joseph Stalin (1879–1953), as Snowball is chased off of the farm by Napoleon—Orwell's stand-in for Stalin. Like Napoleon, Stalin was unconcerned with debates and ideas. Instead, he valued power for its own sake and by 1927 had assumed complete control of the Com-munist Party through acts of terror and brutality. Napoleon's dogs are like Stalin's KGB, his secret police that he used to eliminate all opposi-tion. As Napoleon gains control under the guise of improving the ani-mals' lives, Stalin used a great deal of propaganda—symbolized by Squealer in the novel—to present himself as an idealist working for change. His plan to build the windmill reflects Stalin's Five Year Plan for revitalizing the nation's industry and agriculture. Stalin's ordering Lenin's body to be placed in the shrine-like Lenin's Tomb parallels Napoleon's unearthing of old Major's skull, and his creation of the Order of the Green Banner parallels Stalin's creation of the Order of Lenin. Thanks, in part, to animals like Boxer (who swallow whole all of their leader's lies), Stalin became one of the world's most feared and brutal dictators.

Numerous events in the novel are based on ones that occurred dur-ing Stalin's rule. The Battle of the Cowshed parallels the Civil War that occurred after the 1917 Revolution. Frederick represents Adolf Hitler (1889–1945), who forged an alliance with Stalin in 1939—but who then found himself fighting Stalin's army in 1941. Frederick seems like an ally of Napoleon's, but his forged banknotes reveal his true charac-ter. The confessions and executions of the animals reflect the various purges and "show trials" that Stalin conducted to rid himself of any possible threat of dissention. In 1921, the sailors at the Kronshdadt military base unsuccessfully rebelled against Communist rule, as the hens attempt to rebel against Napoleon. The Battle of the Windmill reflects the U.S.S.R.'s involvement in World War II—specifically the Battle of Stalingrad in 1943, when Stalin's forces defeated Hitler's (as Napoleon's defeat Frederick). Finally, the card game at the novel's end parallels the Tehran Conference (November 28–December 1, 1943), where Stalin, Winston Churchill, and Franklin D. Roosevelt met to discuss the ways to forge a lasting peace after the war—a peace that Orwell mocks by having Napoleon and Pilkington flatter each other and then betray their duplicitous natures by cheating in the card game.

Major Themes of the Novel

Satire is loosely defined as art that ridicules a specific topic in order to provoke readers into changing their opinion of it. By attacking what they see as human folly, satirists usually imply their own opinions on how the thing being attacked can be remedied. Perhaps the most famous work of British satire is Jonathan Swift's *Gulliver's Travels* (1726), where the inhabitants of the different lands Gulliver visits embody what Swift saw as the prominent vices and corruptions of his time. As a child, Orwell discovered and devoured Swift's novel, which became one of his favorite books. Like *Gulliver's Travels*, *Animal Farm* is a satirical novel in which Orwell, like Swift, attacks what he saw as some of the prominent follies of *his* time. These various satirical targets comprise the major themes of Orwell's novel.

The Nature of Tyrants

Broadly speaking, *Animal Farm* satirizes politicians, specifically their rhetoric, ability to manipulate others, and insatiable lust for power. Despite his seemingly altruistic motives, Napoleon is presented as the epitome of a power-hungry individual who masks all of his actions with the excuse that they are done for the betterment of the farm. His stealing the milk and apples, for example, is explained by the lie that these foods have nutrients essential to pigs, who need these nutrients to carry on their managerial work. His running Snowball off the farm is explained by the lie that Snowball was actually a traitor, working for Jones—and that the farm will fare better without him. Each time that Napoleon and the other pigs wish to break one of the Seven Commandments, they legitimize their transgressions by changing the Commandment's original language. Whenever the farm suffers a setback, Napoleon blames Snowball's treachery—which the reader, of course, knows is untrue. Napoleon's walking on two legs, wearing a derby hat, and toasting Pilkington reflect the degree to which he (and the other pigs) completely disregard the plights of the other animals in favor of satisfying their own cravings for power. Thus, the dominant theme of *Animal Farm* is the tendency for those who espouse the most virtuous ideas to become the worst enemies of the people whose lives they are claiming to improve.

The Role of the Populace

Orwell, however, does not imply that Napoleon is the only cause for Animal Farm's decline. He also satirizes the different kinds of people whose attitudes allow rulers like Napoleon to succeed. Mollie, whose only concerns are materialistic, is like people who are so self-centered that they lack any political sense or understanding of what is happening around them. Apolitical people like Mollie—who care nothing for justice or equality—offer no resistance to tyrants like Napoleon. Boxer is likened to the kind of blindly devoted citizen whose reliance on slogans ("Napoleon is always right") prevents him from examining in more detail his own situation: Although Boxer is a sympathetic character, his ignorance is almost infuriating, and Orwell suggests that this unquestioning ignorance allows rulers like Napoleon to grow stronger. Even Benjamin, the donkey, contributes to Napoleon's rise, because his only stand on what is occurring is a cynical dismissal of the facts: Although he is correct in stating that "Life would go on as it had always gone on—that is, badly," he, too, does nothing to stop the pigs' ascension or even raise the other animals' awareness of what is happening. His only action is to warn Boxer of his impending death at the knacker's—but this is futile as it occurs too late to do Boxer any good.

Religion and Tyranny

Another theme of Orwell's novel that also strikes a satiric note is the idea of religion being the "opium of the people" (as Karl Marx famously wrote). Moses the raven's talk of Sugarcandy Mountain originally annoys many of the animals, since Moses, known as a "teller of tales," seems an unreliable source. At this point, the animals are still hopeful for a better future and therefore dismiss Moses' stories of a paradise elsewhere. As their lives worsen, however, the animals begin to believe him, because "Their lives now, they reasoned, were hungry and laborious; Was it not right and just that a better world should exist somewhere else?" Here, Orwell mocks the futile dreaming of a better place that clearly does not exist. The pigs allow Moses to stay on the farm—and even encourage his presence by rewarding him with beer—because they know that his stories of Sugarcandy Mountain will keep the animals docile: As long as there is *some* better world *somewhere*—even after death—the animals will trudge through this one. Thus Orwell implies that religious devotion—viewed by many as a noble character trait—can actually distort the ways in which one thinks of his or her life on earth.

False Allegience

A final noteworthy (and again, satiric) theme is the way in which people proclaim their allegiance to each other, only to betray their true intentions at a later time. Directly related to the idea that the rulers of the rebellion (the pigs) eventually betray the ideals for which they presumably fought, this theme is dramatized in a number of relationships involving the novel's human characters. Pilkington and Frederick, for example, only listen to Jones in the Red Lion because they secretly hope to gain something from their neighbor's misery. Similarly, Frederick's buying the firewood from Napoleon seems to form an alliance that is shattered when the pig learns of Frederick's forged banknotes. The novel's final scene demonstrates that, despite all the friendly talk and flattery that passes between Pilkington and Napoleon, each is still trying to cheat the other (as seen when both play the ace of spades simultaneously). Of course, only one of the two is *technically* cheating, but Orwell does not indicate which one because such a fact is unimportant: The "friendly" game of cards is a facade that hides each ruler's desire to destroy the other.

Thus, as Swift used fantastic places to explore the themes of political corruption in the eighteenth century, so Orwell does with *his* own fantastic setting to satirize the twentieth. According to Orwell, rulers such as Napoleon will continue to grow in number—and in power—unless people become more politically aware and more wary of these leader's "noble" ideals.

CliffsNotes Review

Use this CliffsNotes Review to test your understanding of the original text and reinforce what you've learned in this book. After you work through the review and essay questions, identify the quote section, and the fun and useful practice projects, you're well on your way to understanding a comprehensive and meaningful interpretation of *Animal Farm*.

Q&A

1. Who inspires the animals to begin planning their rebellion?

   a. old Major
   b. Napoleon
   c. Snowball

2. Which one of Snowball's plans is stolen by Napoleon?

   a. an arsenal
   b. a fence
   c. a windmill

3. After Boxer's collapse, he is ___.

   a. comforted by Napoleon
   b. healed by a veterinarian
   c. sold to the knacker's

Answers: (1) a. (2) c. (3) c.

Identify the Quote: Find Each Quote in *Animal Farm*

1. Man is the only real enemy we have. Remove Man from the scene, and the root cause of hunger and overwork is abolished forever.

2. Will there still be sugar after the rebellion?

3. War is war. The only good human being is a dead one.

4. I trust that every animal here appreciates the sacrifice that Comrade Napoleon has made in taking this extra labour upon himself. Do not imagine, comrades, that leadership is a pleasure! On the contrary, it is a deep and heavy responsibility.

5. Do you know the enemy who has come in the night and overthrown our windmill? SNOWBALL!

6. ALL ANIMALS ARE EQUAL / BUT SOME ARE MORE EQUAL THAN OTHERS.

7. If you have your lower animals to contend with . . . we have our lower classes!

Answers: (1) [Old Major, describing his dream.] (2) [Mollie asking Snowball about how she will fare in the rebellion.] (3) [Snowball to Boxer after Boxer fears he has killed the stable-boy.] (4) [Squealer manipulating the animals' perceptions of Napoleon.] (5) [Napoleon after the windmill is toppled in a storm.] (6) [The final revision of the Seventh Commandment of Animalism during Napoleon's rule.] (7) [Pilkington toasting Napoleon in the novel's final scene.]

Essay Questions

1. Compare the lives of the animals when they live under Jones and under Napoleon. In what ways has Napoleon proven himself a similar tyrant?

2. Closely examine old Major's speech to the animals in Chapter 1 and discuss the ways in which he uses language to persuade his listeners.

3. Explain how one of the novel's minor characters (such as Mollie or Moses) illuminates Orwell's major themes and issues.

4. Examine Orwell's tone when describing the way the animals think of themselves under Napoleon's rule: How does Orwell's tone add to the novel's humor?

5. Explain how the human characters contribute to the novel's themes and issues.

6. Based upon *Animal Farm*, what deductions can a reader make about the kind of political system of which Orwell would approve?

Practice Projects

1. Read some of the famous fables by the Greek writer Aesop (sixth century B.C.) and then explain the ways in which Orwell uses elements of the beast-fable in *Animal Farm*. Be sure to explain why, like Aesop, Orwell would employ animals to tell a story about human morality.

2. Research the Russian Revolution of 1917 and create a poster or Web page in which you connect the historical figures to their corresponding characters in *Animal Farm*. Be sure to explain how a certain animal's personality suits its corresponding historical figure. (How, for example, is Napoleon *like* Stalin?)

3. Read Orwell's *Nineteen Eighty-Four* and report on the ways that the novel's vision of a totalitarian state resembles Napoleon's government in *Animal Farm*.

CliffsNotes Resource Center

The learning doesn't need to stop here. CliffsNotes Resource Center shows you the best of the best—links to the best information in print and online about the author and/or related works. And don't think that this is all we've prepared for you; we've put all kinds of pertinent information at www.cliffsnotes.com. Look for all the terrific resources at your favorite bookstore or local library and on the Internet. When you're online, make your first stop www.cliffsnotes.com where you'll find more incredibly useful information about *Animal Farm*.

Books

This CliffsNotes book provides a meaningful interpretation of *Animal Farm*. If you are looking for information about the author and/or related works, check out these other publications:

The Orwell Reader, with an Introduction by Richard H. Rovere. This anthology of Orwell's fiction, essays, and reportage contains generous excerpts from Orwell's novels as well as several important essays, such as, "Why I Write," "Such, Such Were the Joys . . . " and "Politics and the English Language." This book is a great introduction to Orwell's work. New York: Harcourt Brace & Company, 1984.

A Concise History of the Russian Revolution, by Richard Pipes and Peter Dimock. This condensation of Pipes' two-volume history of the Revolution examines Russia under Lenin as well as the rise of the Bolsheviks. One of the book's major arguments is that Russian Communism was doomed from its very beginning. New York: Alfred A. Knopf, 1996.

Orwell: The Authorized Biography, by Michael Sheldon. Shelden's readable and extensive biography details Orwell's childhood at St. Cyprian's, his police career in Burma, his fighting in Spain, and a number of other periods in order to explore the ways that they affected Orwell's writing. Drawing on previously unpublished letters and other writings, Sheldon's book stands as the definitive biography of Orwell. New York; HarperCollins Publishers, 1991.

The Unknown Orwell, by Peter Stansky and William Abrahams. This biography examines Orwell's life as Eric Blair, before he adopted his more famous pseudonym, and draws on interviews with Orwell's sister Avril to re-create his life as a schoolboy and police officer. New York: Alfred A. Knopf, 1972.

It's easy to find books published by Wiley Publishing, Inc. You'll find them in your favorite bookstores (on the Internet and at a store near you). We also have three Web sites that you can use to read about all the books we publish:

■ www.cliffsnotes.com

■ www.dummies.com

■ www.wiley.com

Internet

Check out these Web resources for more information about George Orwell and *Animal Farm*:

The Chestnut Tree Café, www.seas.upenn.edu/~allport/ chestnut/chestnut.htm—This comprehensive and exhaustive site from the University of Pennsylvania hosts a number of essays about Orwell's work, as well as an extensive biography of Orwell and a large FAQ section.

The George Orwell Page, www.k-1.com/orwell—This Austrian site features a number of useful e-texts and links, as well as a visual gallery.

Orwell Discovery. www.chs.edu.sg/~991g16/orwell/intro. htm—This easy-to-navigate site features an *Animal Farm* quiz and a pair of tables linking events from *Animal Farm* to those of the Russian Revolution.

Next time you're on the Internet, don't forget to drop by www. cliffsnotes.com. We created an online Resource Center that you can use today, tomorrow, and beyond.

Films and Audio Recordings

Animal Farm, deRochemont Films, 1954. Directed by John Halas and using the voice talents of Maurice Denham and Gordon Heath, this film follows the events of the novel closely and is marked by almost surreal animation—unlike that found in many children's cartoons.

Animal Farm, Hallmark Entertainment, 1999. Directed by John Stephenson and starring the voices of Kelsey Grammer, Patrick Stewart, and Peter Ustinov. This live-action, made-for-TV adaptation departs from the novel in some critical ways but is marked by its computer graphics, which makes the animals' speaking seem realistic.

Animal Farm, by George Orwell. Audiotape. Read by Timothy West. Penguin USA, 1996. This is one of the many audio versions of the novel.

Send Us Your Favorite Tips

In your quest for knowledge, have you ever experienced that sublime moment when you figure out a trick that saves time or trouble? Perhaps you realized you were taking ten steps to accomplish something that could have taken two. Or you found a little-known workaround that achieved great results. If you've discovered a useful resource that gave you insight into or helped you understand *Animal Farm* and you'd like to share it, the CliffsNotes staff would love to hear from you. Go to our Web site at www.cliffsnotes.com and click the Talk to Us button. If we select your tip, we may publish it as part of CliffsNotes Daily, our exciting, free e-mail newsletter. To find out more or to subscribe to a newsletter, go to www.cliffsnotes.com on the Web.

Index

Check Out the All-New CliffsNotes Guides